370.15

Also in the Learning and Assessment Theory Series

The Theory of Learners Julie Cotton
The Theory of Assessment Julie Cotton
The Theory of Learning Strategies Julie Cotton

The
Theory of
Learning

An Introduction

Julie Cotton

KOGAN
PAGE

London ● Philadelphia

To my brother Roger and my dear husband Chris

First published in 1995

Reprinted 1996

Apart from any fair dealing for the purposes of research or private study, or criticism or review, as permitted under the Copyright Designs and Patents Act, 1988, this publication may only be reproduced, stored or transmitted, in any form or by any means, with the prior permission in writing of the publishers, or in the case of reprographic reproduction in accordance with the terms of licences issued by the Copyright Licensing Agency. Enquiries concerning reproduction outside those terms should be sent to the publishers at the undermentioned address:

Kogan Page Limited
120 Pentonville Road
London N1 9JN

© Julie Cotton, 1995

British Library Cataloguing in Publication Data

A CIP record for this book is available from the British Library

ISBN 0 7494 1480 4

Typeset by Saxon Graphics Ltd, Derby
Printed and bound in Great Britain by
Biddles Ltd, Guildford and King's Lynn

Contents

Introduction   7

Chapter 1   Perception, Attention and Pattern Formation   9

Chapter 2   Memory and Improving Memory   24

Chapter 3   Psychological Perspectives on Learning   40

Chapter 4   Motivation and Goal Clarity   52

Chapter 5   Learning on One's Own   68

Chapter 6   The Role of Language in Learning   80

Chapter 7   Learning a Skill   92

Chapter 8   Experiential Learning   109

Chapter 9   Understanding and Thinking   125

Chapter 10   Problem-solving   140

References   157

Introduction

This book is for every full-time and part-time teacher, including trainers, further education lecturers, work-based skills trainers, higher education lecturers, adult education lecturers, instructors, professors, open-learning managers, tutors, distance learning writers, counsellors, mentors, staff development managers and even, as one of my students called himself, apprentice masters. We are all concerned with the business of helping other people to learn and we may even gain a few tips on how to improve our own learning if we study the theory of learning itself.

The content of this book concentrates on general aspects of learning – the things we all have in common such as perception, memory and recall. The individuality of learners is considered in book two in the series, the strategies for helping other people to learn are covered in book three and the theory of assessment and evaluation is the subject for book four.

After 25 years of training for vocational, technical, higher and adult education I have never come across a book which covers the topic of general learning theory in a user-friendly way. I have had to scour a few general books on psychology, some on philosophy and collect a large number of pickings, even down to leftovers on the photo-copier. Good and helpful books have been written in related fields – such as school teaching and instructions for the armed services – but the field of post-compulsory (school leaving) education seems to be sadly neglected.

In this introductory book I have tried to assume that the reader has nothing but an interest in learning, but it is very difficult to avoid the jargon which bedevils any writing about education and training. I have included a few suggestions for activities which may help you to apply theory to your own work. Without offence to the reader, I hope, I have suggested places where you might stop and have a good think about what the theory means in practice. To this end I have asked some open questions which are intended to trigger your thoughts rather than come to any hard and fast conclusions. You may find the chapters readable in their own right, but I have placed the main concepts at the beginning of each chapter in case you want to use the book as a traditional reference.

Remember that this is only an introduction to the theory of learning and maybe your pet theory is missing! After the first four books in the series I intend to revisit each of the four topics in turn but at a more advanced level of study, so that the second phase of the series will be pitched at graduate level. Some books call themselves an 'Introduction' and they are, in reality, fiendishly complicated, so I hope that I have not indulged in such one-upmanship and you find this book a helpful introduction to the topic of learning.

Chapter 1

Perception, Attention and Pattern Formation

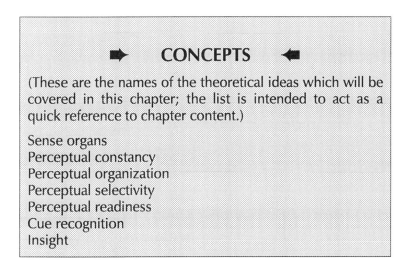

➡ **CONCEPTS** ⬅

(These are the names of the theoretical ideas which will be covered in this chapter; the list is intended to act as a quick reference to chapter content.)

Sense organs
Perceptual constancy
Perceptual organization
Perceptual selectivity
Perceptual readiness
Cue recognition
Insight

INTRODUCTION

Almost all learning starts outside the body, so before we can think about new information it has to pass through our sense organs, nerves and on to the brain. Some of our sense organs are better at recording information than others; the sense of smell, for example, is especially efficient. As well as fluctuations in the efficiency of our sense organs, the information which finally reaches the brain is filtered by our own personality; we all moderate what our sense organs

9

record according to what we want to 'see' and what we want to avoid. In other words, nothing enters our brain without being affected by the working of our bodies, called physiology, and the working of our mind, called psychology. In the first two chapters I will introduce you to some basic principles of physiology and psychology which are important in learning.

SENSE ORGANS

The sense organs record touch, sight, taste, hearing and smell with the sense of smell as probably the best recording instrument: the human nose can detect differences in fragrance of just a few parts in a million and this accuracy gives the perfume industry a few problems. All the senses including touch, hearing and sight play a part in the learning process and it is regrettable that our best sense organ plays such a limited part in general learning. When I use pictures, words and objects to touch for the explanation of a new idea, how I wish it had a good strong smell to make the idea really memorable!

Have you noticed how often people close their eyes when they are performing very delicate operations by touch? My father always stood in front of the mirror and then closed his eyes before he tied his tie when dressing for work. Little children seem to screw their eyes up particularly tightly and often show the effort of concentration even more by letting a bit of tongue slip out of the side of their mouths. We cut out the input from other senses when we want to take notice of incoming information about touch, feel and sensation.

With sound, people seem to use one of two different sense recording systems in the brain; some appear to record the noise from the sense of hearing and 'replay' what was heard like a tape recorder working inside the head. This is called the 'inner ear' and a person using this mechanism can play back to check what the noise sounded like. Others seem to translate noise into written text, which is a much more visual way of recording what was heard. This visual processing is called the 'inner eye' and a person using this method will repeat a word definition of what was heard rather than attempt to repeat the sounds. Like most thinking or cognitive processes, both systems are available to us but each individual seems to have a preference for one method or the other.

Sight dominates our senses but, as a recording instrument, eyes are not very accurate. There are some common problems which are due to physiology and not psychology; for example, each eye has a 'blind spot' at the site where the optic nerve enters the back of the eye; even when we look with one eye at a time and the blind patch ought to be clear, we do not notice this flaw. Some people can be colour blind; this is more likely in men. All of us only have colour vision when we look ahead because everything round the edge of our visual field is in black and white. Sometimes it is important to know how far away something is; sailors call it 'distance off' when referring to the coastline. We guess the distance off from our record of height recorded in the eye so that the smaller the recorded height the further the distance away. This rough measure is sufficient when we are distinguishing between a mouse and an elephant, but recent research has shown that more children than adults are involved in street accidents because children are perceived as being further away than they really are when their shorter height makes a shorter image in the car driver's eye.

Sense organs are important in learning because they are the only way that we can record and observe the world outside our own bodies. If we are aware of the limitations and defects of our senses we can make better decisions about the accuracy of what is happening 'out there'.

ACTIVITY

See your blind spot
Take a piece of paper and draw a little cross in the centre. About four inches to the right of the central cross draw a little 'Y'. Cover the left eye with your left hand and hold the paper at arm's length away from

your right eye. Look at the little cross in the centre of the paper and gradually pull the paper forwards towards your right eye. As you continue to stare at the cross note what happens to the 'Y' mark. Yes – it really does disappear and reappear; no excuses: if you don't see this effect you will just have to do the experiment again!

How do you feel?
Touch can be very important when learning skills, so identify a skill at work where touch is important. Try to run through the skill, first with your eyes open and then with your eyes shut. Do you detect any difference? You might be able to use a heightened awareness of touch when helping other people to learn a skill.

How do you hear?
Stop and listen to a noise and afterwards recall the noise in your mind. Now decide if you heard the sound in your 'inner ear' like the playing of a tape recorder or if you recall the noise as words by using your 'inner eye'. You may find that you have to do this exercise once or twice because it is surprisingly difficult to concentrate at first.

Can you use taste to teach?
The sense of taste can only record four things: acid, sweet, bitter and salt. I once taught students in the catering industry to distinguish between simple sugars by taste. These white substances look very much alike but they are easy to distinguish by taste: for example, fructose, the fruit sugar, is very sweet and sharp but the milk sugar, lactose, seems hardly sweet at all. I have known lessons on acidity start with the sucking of acid drops but you may have difficulty thinking of ways of using the sense of taste because you do not want to poison the learners.

Checking the range of colour vision
Stand up and look straight in front of you. Hold your arms out sideways and waggle your hands up and down. Gradually move your arms forward until your

hands come within sight. Don't forget to keep looking forward. Think about how your hands look. Are they in colour or do you have to turn your head to look at your hands before you have colour vision? Again, you will have to concentrate on this effect but it is possible to notice that the edges of our visual field are indeed in black and white.

Tracking with the eyes

Finally, and you will need another person to help you see this effect, let us look at how the eye only records the visual scene when it rests steadily on an object. The best way of showing this is to let the eye follow a moving object when it is focused on the object but the background passes in a blur. Sit opposite another person and ask them to follow the movement of the top of a pen as you move the pen slowly across his or her field of vision. As you watch the other person's eyes you will see that the movement is very smooth and continuously changing. Now ask the other person to repeat the same eye movement without the moving pen. It is impossible to recreate smooth eye movements without the moving object and the eyes move in small jerky steps from one focus position to the next. This is why all people playing ball games are told to 'Keep your eye on the ball'; once you have lost sight of the moving object your eyes jump about until they find the ball and when they do make contact they have to change quickly into the continuous tracking movement again.

So far I have described ways in which our perception is affected by the purely mechanical limitations of the way our body functions; now let us look at how our own mind can make assumptions about incoming information. Sometimes these assumptions are useful and save us time; for example, we don't have to look at every piece of office furniture before we know that we are in our own office! On other occasions, we may jump to a conclusion too quickly and fail to recognize changes when they have occurred.

PERCEPTUAL CONSTANCY

Normal living would be impossible if we could not make assumptions that things, generally, remain the same. If we were to wake up each morning and have to guess which side of the sky the sun came up we would not have any time left over to carry out the normal jobs of living. We need to work in a constant framework and so we interpret the information from our sense organs with a bias towards constancy.

Shape constancy is a good example; when we look at a round plate our eyes will only record a complete circle if we stand directly in front of the plate. From every other viewpoint the image of the plate on the eye is elliptical. Unless we try to look at the plate so that we can draw it, our mind will always register plates as constantly round even though we hardly ever record a really round shape in the eye. The same is true of:

- colour – a white dress is recorded as white in the mind even though it is grey to the eye in most lights
- brightness – an area of brightness, like the sky near the sunset, is seen as bright even though the twilight fades to darkness and the eye can hardly see
- size – an object, like a tree, is seen as tall even though it may be a tiny dot on the horizon.

Perceptual constancy is such a common and everyday experience that you might be tempted to think of this interpretation of incoming information as a function of physiology, but it is not. We do not see round plates, we normally see elliptical plates, but our minds – psychologically – insist that elliptical plates are round.

PERCEPTUAL ORGANIZATION

Some early researchers, collectively known as the 'Gestalt school', suggested some general rules of how we organize

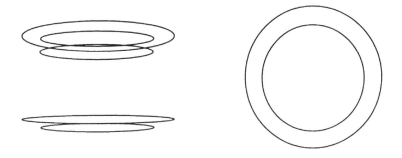

Figure 1.1   *Plates are always round*

incoming information and these simple rules are very help-ful in understanding perception. The word 'Gestalt' does not have a clear translation into English but conveys the mean-ing of 'a wholeness' or grasping the overall significance of a situation. It is sometimes expressed in English as 'the whole being greater than the sum of the parts'. Here are short explanations of each of the four methods of organization.

Similarity

We tend to put things together if they are alike so that when we look at the cars in a car park we might summarize by saying, 'There are five Rovers, three Fords and one BMW'. It is easy to lump information together by putting things into classes and this principle is the basis of descrip-tive statistics which works with organization by *similarity*. Most people find this type of organization very useful as a way of handing lots of information but you must remem-ber that it is a personal choice when we decide how to select for the categories and this selection can be biased to suit a desired statistical result.

Proximity

The second principle of organization put forward by the Gestalt school is *proximity*, when we put things together because they are close to each other. For example, we link places together because they are geographically close, like 'Greater Manchester', or we link experiences and ideas together if they occur closely in time. Association of ideas is a very old principle of learning and it is based on organization through proximity so that a teacher or trainer will link ideas and examples in close proximity. The proximity organization principle is behind both the use of visual and sound aids to try to build learning links and the use of an overview, called an 'advanced organizer', at the start of a new topic. Both techniques help the learner to slot new information into a clear learning structure and to make sure that ideas and examples are 'stored' close together in the memory.

```
x  x  x  x  x  x  x  x
x  x  x  x  x  x  x  x
```

THESE ARE ROWS AND ...

```
x  x  x  x  x  x
x  x  x  x  x  x
x  x  x  x  x  x
```

... THESE ARE COLUMNS

Figure 1.2 *Proximity*

Continuity

This is a more difficult principle to explain. When we are presented with a mass of information we try to look for simple patterns to help us to organize and untangle what seems to be a senseless heap of information. When presented with what is called 'information overload' we have to look for a common trend or a standard which will help us to put the whole thing into a simpler structure. The task of making order out of chaos is an essential skill for the instructor or teacher of practical subjects; it is one of the greatest challenges in most skill and competency training to help a learner to solve problems. The key technique in problem solving is to isolate the essential nature of, or general rule which underlies, a particular practical example. The learner has to be helped to see an overall continuous pattern in a mass of examples and it is very important to pick the right theme because future learning can be damaged if the instructor fails to spot a 'better fit' or a more elegant solution to the information.

Closure

This fourth organizational principle is again quite tricky to explain but it is rather like the work of the cartoon artist. Just as we see a whole picture from a few lines in a drawing, we leap to a whole idea or sum up a whole situation sometimes from very little information at all. If you put three unconnected lines in the rough plan of a triangle on a piece of paper, the mind will record what the eye sees as a triangle. In other words, we have a tendency to complete and fill in observed information to make a pattern which we already recognize.

The principle of 'closure' can be very useful. For example, I recognize my husband immediately by minimal information such as two treads on the stairs or one cough. This

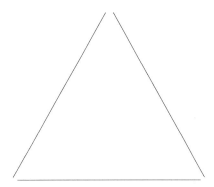

Figure 1.3 *Is this a triangle?*

familiarity can be dangerous. Let us take the case of a medical doctor and the treatment of his or her immediate family when this very process of closure prevents the observation of change. I have a doctor friend who was working in a remote part of Africa and it was only when a fellow medical doctor came to visit that it was observed that the whole family was yellow with jaundice.

⇨ **STOP AND REFLECT** ⇦

When a learner is starting on a new subject it is very difficult to know what to look at and how to recognize, say, the parts of a machine. How do you define new subjects to students so that they recognize and select what they are supposed to be seeing?

How do you provide a framework or advanced organizer for your learners to use as a reference when you introduce a new topic?

How do you present underlying rules and principles in your subject area so that your students can see the 'continuity of the theory' in a mass of problems?

PERCEPTUAL SELECTIVITY

We have so much information coming in from the outside world that we cannot pay attention to all of it and we have to be selective. The sense organs send a continuous stream of information to the brain and it is one of the characteristics of human beings that we pay attention to what we want to see and hear and ignore the rest of the information. This is called 'perceptual selectivity'.

ACTIVITY

Work through your sense organs and jot down the information which is being fed to your brain at the present while you read this page. You should find that it forms quite a collection of sights, sounds, smells, tastes and sensations.

PERCEPTUAL READINESS

Our personality and personal experience influence the way we interpret what we see. Here are some of the factors.

Knowledge and interest

When I walk down the street with my husband we see different things because we are influenced by our own knowledge and interest. I am keen on gardening and so I automatically record plants, shrubs and trees. Chris is a surveyor and he observes and possibly values all the buildings so that he notices the construction fabrics and assesses the age of the buildings by the arches over the windows and positioning of door openings. Everyone chooses a different selection from the available information and interprets this information in a different way to come to unique, individual conclusions.

Previous experience

Previous experience can warp the way in which a person perceives a new situation. If a pedestrian falls against the side of a car in the street, all observers will be influenced by what they have seen before. The health professional may see a person having a heart attack, the policeman may see someone trying to break into a car and the party-goer may see a fellow drunk who has been to a good party.

Personality traits

The many variations in personality will be considered later in the series but it is worth noting now that each person has an independent approach to perception. One person may look on the bright side and see only excellent and cheerful outcomes, whereas another may take a pessimistic view of the same experience. Both an optimistic and a pessimistic temperament can be turned into effective teaching in the following ways. The cheerful teacher who sees all 'the geese as swans' may perceive a learner as having positive responses and a good potential talent and, with this encouragement, the learner who is lacking in confidence can take a more positive view of his or her own potential and begin to work effectively and successfully. On the other hand, a more pessimistic, serious trainer can help a careless learner to work with precision and this can be just the right approach to help the learner to take the work seriously and pay proper attention to detail.

Social and cultural influence

Social learning is one of the most potent influences on training and teaching. Culture may influence the way in which a trainer or a learner views a particular role. A boy's success at engineering may have nothing to do with his innate ability to master differential calculus but a great deal to do with his trainer's readiness to see him, because he is a boy, as a budding engineer. To a large extent we live up to the expectations of others and, for example, a great deal of pressure can be put on young girls by the readiness of teachers to see them as caring and gentle practitioners.

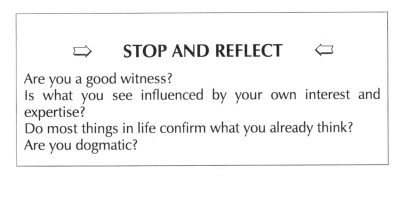

⇨　　**STOP AND REFLECT**　　⇦

Are you a good witness?
Is what you see influenced by your own interest and expertise?
Do most things in life confirm what you already think?
Are you dogmatic?

Functional fixedness

If you take a particular view by virtue of your knowledge, past experience, personality or socio/cultural influences you could be prone to *functional fixedness*. This 'fate' awaits those who are incapable of moving from a fixed position when new evidence is presented; in fact it is the basis of prejudice and tunnel vision (the inability to be deflected from a very straight line of reasoning). Teachers do not want to be so adaptable that they lack respect for quality and good standards, but, equally, they do not want to be so rigid that they can not accept any change.

ACTIVITY

It is important that the trainer or teacher learns about his or her own strengths and weaknesses. A realistic and practical assessment of one's own personality and interests makes it much easier to help and understand learners. This activity is introspective so do not let it become a confession session! We are only looking at perceptual readiness. Jot down a few notes in answer to the following questions:

How might your own knowledge base and interests affect your perception of events?
Think about your previous experience and ask yourself if there are any events which might distort your perception?
What sort of a person are you? Does this affect your assessment of other people?
Do the influences of your cultural or social background limit the amount of help you can give to a learner?

CUE RECOGNITION

This is the very stuff of learning a skill or of learning to be competent. For example, when an engine cover is taken off to reveal an engine, to a novice it might as well be so much metal spaghetti, or if you place a new trainee in a commercial selling situation, many of the subtle complexities go straight over his or her head. In each case you have to know what to look for.

There are three parts to a practical skill:

- Cognitive skill – having a certain amount of knowledge.
- Psycho-motor skill – carrying out the physical task.
- Perceptual skill – judging good work and recognizing defects.

If you are familiar with a subject or skill it is extremely difficult to appreciate the lack of knowledge and understanding of someone who is new to the skill. There will be much more on this topic in this book and in the series, but it is important to note at this stage that perceptual skills are essential for good practice and for judging the quality of the end product.

Picking out the key points in a process makes it easy to identify the cues which must be recognized. Much of practical learning is the fitting together of cues which stimulate responses which again become the cue to the next response. This traditional training linkage of stimulus and response is the underpinning of much skill development.

The cue or stimulus response mechanism is a basis for a school of psychology called 'Behaviourism'. We will cover the various schools of psychology which affect learning later in the series. It is worth noting at this stage that cue recognition and the expected response can be formed into a quick series of actions which make up very swift physical skills. Each stage of these series or 'closed loops' becomes automatic as one cue recognition follows another.

INSIGHT

Many phrases used to descibe the sensation of sudden insight into understanding refer to the sense organs and they are all used to describe the 'wholeness' of Gestalt. Here are a few examples and you can probably add many of your own:

' ...seen the light'
' ...the penny drops'
' ...an ahha experience'
'Hello – here come the thing-a-me-bobs again'
'EUREKA!'

When this sudden realization of understanding is experienced, every observation and fact seems to fit into place; they form a pattern so that much complex and sophisticated understanding can be built on the stepping stones of insight. The teacher and trainer can encourage insight for the learner by giving an overview or advanced organizer before starting on a new topic.

ACTIVITY

Plan an advanced organizer for the next topic you are going to introduce to your learners and then check that you can introduce each new idea to the learner who has no experience of the subject.

Chapter 2

Memory and Improving Memory

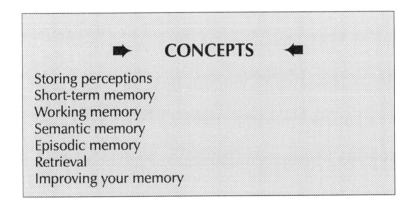

➡️ **CONCEPTS** ⬅️

Storing perceptions
Short-term memory
Working memory
Semantic memory
Episodic memory
Retrieval
Improving your memory

STORING PERCEPTIONS

Let us look at what happens to the images, sounds, smells, tastes and sensations which we pick up from the outside world. These perceptions are not a true representation of what is 'out there' because they have already been distorted by our own levels of attention, interest, previous knowledge and social and cultural bias. These personalized impressions enter our private world and seem to be received by our 'inner voice', 'inner eye' and 'inner ear'. I suppose that we must also have an 'inner nose', 'inner taste buds' and 'inner skin sensation' and we will think about these a little later.

When someone tells you a funny story you may repeat the last line to yourself just to make sure that you don't forget; if you look up a telephone number you may repeat the number to yourself as you walk to the phone to dial. This is the work of the inner voice. The rehearsal of what you want to remember needs some attention and concentration so you do not want to be interrupted by any disturbing noise. It is sometimes easier to concentrate if you do not use the inner voice alone but speak the line or the number out loud. When children are learning to read they seem to go through a stage when this verbalizing is helpful. There is some evidence that reading by using the inner voice is relatively modern and that in the olden days everyone who could read, read aloud.

Some people have excellent inner eyes. My room-mate at university could study textbooks and commit whole pages to memory; I am sure that she could turn over pages and read from her inner eye a textbook in the middle of an examination. Without rehearsal the picture in the inner eye fades in about a second but you can hold the image for longer periods if you continuously run your inner eye over the scene. This picture store seems to be separate from the inner voice and inner ear and you may be able to use the *iconic* or visual memory to overcome interference in the sound field.

Images in the inner ear fade a little more slowly than images in the inner eye; probably you will find that it takes two or even three seconds before the sound memory fades. You can also rehearse the words with the inner voice or concentrate on reminding yourself of the noise if you have a preference for audio memories; if you choose, the inner ear can play whole orchestral works inside your head without the aid of a personal tape recorder. Nobody knows that there is a musical, colourful, adventure going on inside your head unless you give yourself away by a secret little smile or by regular nodding of the head to some internal music.

Not much has been written about inner noses, inner taste buds and inner skin sensations. Smells linger but that is because the molecules are still present. Taste lingers too for the same reason but you can imagine taste and smell. A gourmet can set the digestive juices flowing in his or her mouth by thinking about a favourite dish so I suppose we do have inner taste. Skin sensors of touch do go on recording touch stimuli for quite a long time; this can be up to 10 or 12 seconds after the event. The specialized pressure-recording cells in the skin do seem to have a slow recovery rate.

SHORT-TERM MEMORY

The gap between the recording of sensations from the outside world and the long-term storage of procedures and facts is called the 'short-term memory'; STM for short. Experiments on STM are some of the earliest in the field of psychology. People taking part in these early experiments learnt long lists of nonsense syllables and were then asked to recall the syllables after different lapses of time. To prevent the use of the inner voice to 'practise' in his or her head while they waited to be asked to repeat the nonsense syllables, the person was given a random number immediately after the end of the syllable list and asked to count backwards, aloud, in threes from the random number. This is an interesting experiment because it shows up clearly how we all 'practise' using our inner voice when we want to keep fresh something held in our short-term memory before we use the information – like remembering a car number before writing the number down. You can see the separate nature of the inner eye and the inner voice if you remember a picture – say, of the car number – and you may find that you do not need so much rehearsal before you record the number in writing.

Another result of these early experiments on memory showed the very limited number of things that we can hold in our STM. It seems that everyone can remember between five and nine bits of information in the short-term memory. Look at this string of numbers:

5 9 0 1 4 6 6 8 7 1 3 4 7 1 1 0 8 3 5 7 1 0 6 3 0 1 8 3 2 9 1 5

If this is read out to a group of people who are asked to recall it immediately some common factors will emerge:

- most people will remember 5 9 because these numbers come first; this effect is called 'primacy'
- most people will remember 1 5 or 9 1 5 because these are the last numbers; this effect is called 'recency'
- many people will remember the 'double 6' and the 'double 1' because these form a 'chunk' of information which is memorable as a unit
- some will recognize 4 7 1 1 as a well-known perfume and this will be remembered as a chunk of information too
- individuals might recognize other combinations of numbers which they pick out by familiarity as a single item of information. Your telephone number might be 8 3 5 7 and that to you would be easily memorable.

Here is a summary:

- Short-term memory is very limited.
- The first bit of information presented is easier to recall.
- The last bit of information presented is easier to recall.
- Short-term memory can be enlarged if information is linked together into a few 'chunks'.

These findings are important when information is presented to the learner and they can also help to improve your own memory. First try the activities so that you can enjoy some of these experiences for yourself.

ACTIVITY

Witnesses
Ask three colleagues or friends to describe an experience that they have all witnessed. Make careful notes of each account. If you can't manage to do this try to listen to, or read, two or three different eye-witness accounts about a particular news item.

Looking
Many people do not watch very carefully but they can be taught to sharpen their visual perception. Take a piece of paper and a pencil or pen and sketch something for about five minutes; choose anything: a

person, a flower, a piece of machinery or a building. The object is to learn to look hard at visual detail. You may need to have several attempts at drawing and observing.

When you have finished your sketch, close your eyes and look at the detail you now have in your mind's eye.

Listening

Many people are also very careless listeners. The 'Cocktail party effect' refers to the fact that if someone mentions your name or another piece of information that is of particular interest to you, you will notice. You can catch in on any interesting snippet of other people's conversation even though lots of other talk is going on all around.

Listening to the feedback from a learner is important if you are going to help learning. Try to practise accurate listening by rehearsing what someone else has just said to you using either your inner ear or your inner voice.

How do you record perceptions?

You can check your preferred method of encoding information consciously by asking yourself the following questions:

- How much detail do I record in my inner eye?
- When someone else speaks do I use my inner ear or my inner voice?
- Can I use my inner taste buds and nose to make my saliva run?
- How do I remember touch and sensation?

WORKING MEMORY

The working memory is at the centre of activated knowledge. As information comes in from the environment outside, the working memory has two choices of action: either the information can be stored away in a library or, if it is recognized as being of practical use, it can be docketed for future actions. This means that there are at least two types of long-term memory; a reference library and techniques for practical tasks.

Although a lot of experimental work is being done on brain function at the present time, the exact mechanisms of the mind are not fully understood. There is certainly a storage memory and many attempts have been made to describe how it works. It must contain some type of organization or system and the idea of a pigeonhole system goes back to the ancient Greeks. As far as learning is concerned it seems to be important that new knowledge information should be associated with existing knowledge. The instructor or teacher can do a great deal to help the learner to slot new information into memory by associating it with what has already been learnt.

The working memory can push new information into another type of long-term memory and this is usually called the 'procedural memory'. We seem to have a long-term memory for 'how to do things'. New observations and information from outside may give clues for better ways to carry out tasks. The working memory recognizes such information and slips it into the existing procedural rules. This methodology memory is constantly improved and refined as we plan future actions and think about the best way to go about a task. I think that there is a difference between fantasy and daydreaming. 'When I win the lottery I will...' may lead to pleasant thoughts but it is not very useful. However, down-to-earth, practical daydreaming is a form of forward planning and can improve practical skills and actions very substantially.

SEMANTIC MEMORY

Language is very important in the passing on and storage of knowledge. It has been suggested that language is so important in the process of passing on ideas from one person to another that the 'the limit of language is the limit of thought'. But this suggestion means that language can cover all knowledge of skills and actions in our procedural memory. Words are a very inadequate method of describing the beauty of dancing or the sound of music. However, whether you give language such an all-embracing role or not, everyone does seem to have a word store for memory and this is called the 'semantic memory'.

This memory seems to be based on a library classification system and it is fascinating to think that my bookshelves are labelled in English and my friend Knut's are in German; the language can be important in storing knowledge. So much scientific and technical development has taken place in English-speaking countries that other languages may not have enough specific words to represent the concepts which need to be stored. Some languages have better words than others. There are two separate words for 'to know' in French which are very useful in distinguishing between knowing as recognizing and knowing as understanding. There was a stage in the development of organic chemistry when a student wishing to study the subject had to have a working knowledge of German. However, the English language has a legendary range and capacity and other languages may have to borrow English words to express concepts. It might be described as the French problem of trying to stamp out 'le weekend'.

Again there is research in this area which may well help us to understand the system of association of words a little more easily. DO Hebb (1949) was a man of great vision when he described the loops of memory association in the mind. Recent research appears to prove that Hebb was right; there does seem to be a change in the nature of the protein in the cells of the brain when memory loops of association are formed.

EPISODIC MEMORY

This form of long-term memory is very useful if you have lost something. We seem to remember in long strings connected by time. We can run through the day's events in sequence or we can reflect on a year or a lifetime and all the episodes and experiences are linked by time.

This memory is very useful for helping to fill in gaps. Suppose I have lost my car keys. I must have put them somewhere during the day, but where and when? It is very easy to start to cross-examine myself and work through the day. 'Now, I got up this morning...', I say to myself and it really is not too difficult a task to remember a large amount of detail using time as a prompt.

Although the idea of 'exercising' the brain by, for example, the learning of algebra is very unfashionable these days, there is a great deal to be said for insisting on tidy memory habits as you grow older. The episodic memory is helpful if we want to remember everyday facts when we are at the age when we say things like, 'My memory is starting to go...'. We can start an internal discipline of insisting on the use of episodic memory to make sure that we remember and use the right name or word.

RETRIEVAL

The retrieval process is one of taking knowledge from the long-term memory systems and making it active again. In the case of the procedural memory this active knowledge will lead to actions. Hopefully the actions we carry out will be better considered and more effective after the influx of new information and the modification which has gone on during practical daydreaming processes. The storage memory will be pulled into active knowledge by the association of words or memories triggered by a time search from the episodic memory. This type of active knowledge will be used internally as material for thinking or it will be expressed by the words, gestures and expressions which we declare to the outside world.

In learning theory we have the problem of forgetfulness. It is very rare that all memory is completely wiped out but memory can be very difficult to bring back into the active state of knowledge needed by the working memory. Some instructors and teachers mistake forgetting for not having learned in the first place. One of the things that irritates me most about some teachers can be summed up as, 'You must remember (know) that, I told you so'. Given the vagaries of attention, interest and personal selection of what we perceive in the first place, the teacher might very well have been primarily responsible for the forgetfulness by making the lesson so very boring.

The efficiency of retrieval

Recall is the most efficient sort of remembering because the retrieval is achieved with no hints at all. This is remembering from a standing start. You want a piece of knowledge and up it pops into the working memory all ready for use. As I get older I get quite a buzz from that sort of internal efficiency.

Recognition is the next most effective form of remembering. A lot of negative criticism is made of objective item testing because this tests remembering by recognition. The candidate is asked to recognize the correct answer from a short selection of possible alternatives. Such criticism may not be justified because research shows a strong link between good recall and good recognition. In addition, recognition is a skill that we often use when making choices in everyday living.

Relearning, reconstruction and even remembering only when we have revisited the same context or state as the earlier experience are all less efficient forms of remembering. These types of retrieval show that memory is seldom completely extinguished. An older learner may relearn a little more quickly than someone starting from scratch. If it is really important, perhaps for psychological reasons, that early memories are reconstructed then the techniques of going back to the original place or reliving the original feelings are available.

⇨ **STOP AND REFLECT** ⇦

Can you carry out effective thinking while you are busy in the daytime, or do you set aside special times such as long journeys, before you go to sleep or quiet periods at the weekend?

Do you need a thinking time without interruptions or do your ideas develop when you talk to other people?

Are you sometimes surprised by what you hear yourself saying aloud?

IMPROVING YOUR MEMORY

Some very successful books and programmes have been produced in this field. People like to be thought of as having a good memory in the same way that they wish to be considered slim, vigorous, healthy and attractive. Most of the advice is sound and is usually based on well-known theory.

Here is a list of descriptions and activities that you can try, then select the most useful for yourself and your learners.

ACTIVITY

Improving your memory

Associations

There are many ways in which you can make verbal associations. Write down examples of the following verbal associations from your special area of interest:

a) Group names together – like the names of countries.
b) Make up pairs of words – like knife and fork.
c) Link words which have closeness – like position or sequence.
d) Make opposite associated pairs – like chalk and cheese.
e) Make up a little story to include all the words you want to associate.

Make associations by using your inner eye:

a) Put things together and then visualize the picture.

b) Imagine a place such as a workshop and place in it the things which you want to remember.

c) Make a list and then visualize the words so that you can read the list from memory.

Repetitions

a) Write out what you want to remember a number of times.

b) Repeat out loud what you want to remember a number of times.

c) Listen to a tape recording a number of times.

d) Read what you want to remember a number of times.

Self-testing

Many years ago one of my tutors taught me a very effective way of testing myself when I need to remember a large number of facts; it is called 'the simplest teaching machine in the world'. Take a piece of A4 paper and draw a line straight down the middle of the page. On the left-hand side you write the answers to a series of short questions and write the questions opposite to each answer down the right-hand side. Take a large envelope which just fits the flat paper. At the top right hand side of the envelope cut out a small rectangle up to the centre line. The purpose of the cut-away section is to expose the first question without being able to see the first answer when you place the question and answer sheet into the envelope. Self-testing then becomes easy and you quickly learn not to cheat yourself. Place the sheet in the envelope to expose the first question. Write down the answer and then pull the sheet a little further out so that you can check the first answer to make sure that it is right. Write down the answer to the second question.

I recommend that you try this simple method of helping memory. I believe that I got 17 students of anatomy and physiology through a stiff examination by this method alone.

34

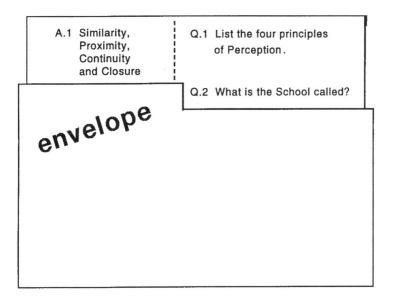

Figure 2.1 *The simplest teaching machine in the world*

Part learning

This is the old method so often used in learning poetry: learn the first line and repeat it and then learn the second line and repeat the first and second line together. Then learn the third line and repeat the first, second and third lines. This process is continued and can be used to learn individual complete verses before putting all the verses together as a final practice.

Rhyme rules

This type of memorization is often illustrated by the rhyme, 'Thirty days hath September...'. You may be clever enough to write some equally useful verses. I was interested to hear that many children in Germany and Holland do not remember the number of days in a month by this method but they do have a visual and touch system worked out on the knuckles of each hand. The knuckle tops are full months and the hollows in between are the shorter ones.

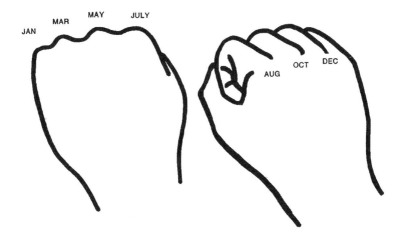

Figure 2.2 *Months on knuckles have 31 days*

The two full months of July and August represent the change over from left hand to right hand.

First letter mnemonics and other short-cuts

Many people remember the colour of the spectrum by the mnenomic Richard Of York Gained Battles In Vain to recall the colours Red, Orange, Yellow, Green, Blue, Indigo, Violet. You may like to compose a similar mnemonic for remembering key points.

There are variations on this theme which can be helpful. Management students remember 'SMART' for objective setting. This stands for Specific, Measurable, Agreed, Realistic and Time-related, or you might have 'KISS' which stands for keep it short and simple. These types of reminders are popular. You will also find expressions such as 'All you need to remember is the 3 Cs or the 5 Fs'.

Perhaps the trainer should use a little caution and avoid too many such aids but I have always been grateful to my first chemistry master for encouraging us to yell out the magic words, 'HeLiBeBCNOF' and 'NeNaMgAlSiPSCl' because I have been able to sort out the periodic classification of chemical elements easily ever since.

Spelling associations

There are many aids to memory in this area. A simple example would be remembering the difference between stationary as applied to cars and stationery as applied to envelopes.

Memory systems

Many of the entertainers who perform as memory men or women use a rhyming number-word association system. The numbers are first associated with a set word and this association is thoroughly learned. The sequence usually goes, 'one is a bun, two is a shoe, three is a tree...' and so on. Some systems rely on number-word rhyme associations which go into several hundreds. Having learned the basic association then any information can be linked to the rhyme word. The first thing you want to remember is linked clearly to the word 'bun' and the second thing you want to remember is linked to the word 'shoe'. The more lurid or rude your personal associations between the number rhyme word and what you want to remember, the more memorable and long-lasting the association! Don't tell anyone else what associations you are making. One of my students committed this error when describing the method and I then had serious trouble with the Equal Opportunities Committee.

Networks of memory patterns

There are several expressions which have been coined from this description of the links and chains of memory associations in the brain. Some call it a 'mind map', others refer to an 'organic diagram', a 'spider diagram' or an 'association diagram'. This type of network represents what goes on inside the brain. We seem to be able to process in series as well as in parallel. If you take the word 'canary', one set of memories will trigger off in a line and run along as canary-bird-animal-living and at the same time the word 'canary' can trigger off laterally and go for canary-colour, canary-football team, canary-island and so on. Take a large piece of paper and write down these lines and spreads of association. You can create a network of crossed associations.

This method is excellent for planning a report or an essay and it is also useful planning for management organization. It is a written description of all that you can remember about a particular subject and is a great help in organizing your thoughts.

Finally let us summarize the conditions for good recall:

- try to avoid making mistakes
- insist on getting into the habit of successful recall
- remember you tend to recall the beginning and end more clearly
- the more you test yourself the better you remember
- the more you concentrate and attend the better you recall

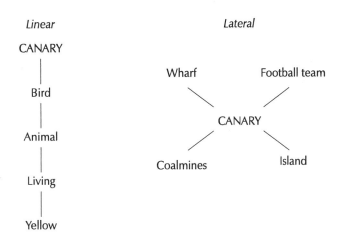

Figure 2.3 *A network of memory patterns*

- the more important the knowledge is to you the better you remember
- the more you associate and relate new knowledge the better
- your recall will be affected by your attitudes and emotions at the time of first perception.

Chapter 3

Psychological Perspectives on Learning

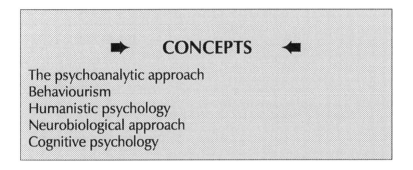

➡ **CONCEPTS** ⬅

The psychoanalytic approach
Behaviourism
Humanistic psychology
Neurobiological approach
Cognitive psychology

There are five major theoretical approaches in psychology. Psychologists tend to become committed to one approach or 'school' of psychology. It is rather like being a committed Christian or a committed Buddhist. If you study human behaviour for a long time you become attached to a particular set of beliefs and convictions. This means that your approach to a topic – like learning – will come from your own particular perspective. Learning might be seen as:

- a simple process of instruction, demonstration and practice
- a question of nerve fibres and brain cells
- a case of maximizing individual potential.

We teachers, trainers, lecturers and instructors do not need to take sides in any discussion. We can look at all the suggested ideas, see the advantages and disadvantages of each one in practice and then use the best approaches for the learning task in hand.

In this chapter we will look at all five approaches so as to get a balanced picture. We need to know about all the methods of presenting information to a learner before we can isolate the few useful techniques for our own subject or field. In just the same way, we need to consider the whole range of psychological approaches to learning before we can select the ones which are useful to us in practice. I will try to give short, easy to read descriptions and if a particular approach seizes your imagination, the libraries are full of splendid books in all these areas.

THE PSYCHOANALYTIC APPROACH

No description of theory in psychology is complete without Freud. Two of his contempories, Jung and Adler, or even Herbart, would say that this is unfair but Freud has become synonymous with 'head-shrinkers' in the popular imagination. His theories have been highly influential in past decades but they seem to have less influence nowadays.

Freud put forward the idea that the individual human being was in conflict due to the demands made by different parts of the personality. These components of personality were the:

- *Id* – a basic, instinctive force which expresses itself either as Eros, the love instinct, with an energy referred to as 'libido', or as Thanatos, the destructive or death instinct.
- *Superego* – a basic, instinctive force which is a drive towards the individual's ideal self. This super conscientiousness is equally as extreme as the id.
- *Ego* – this part of the personality sits between instinctive forces of the superego and the id and tries to keep a balance.

The well-adjusted individual maintains a reasonable balance and so it is presumably this state which is needed to achieve the conditions for successful learning. Freud did not write very much about education but some of his followers tried to use Freudian principles with young children. We may not find much guidance here for successful learning. It is in the field of clinical psychology that this theory has proved to be most successful.

Unless it forms a special part of teaching in, say, psychiatric nursing, it is best to avoid psychoanalysis. There is a temptation for the novice to grab a whole lot of long new words and experiment with playing therapist. This can be extremely dangerous for the learner and could cause permanent damage by meddling in an unknown area. I leave psychoanalysis to the experts. When the mood of my learners starts to become introspective and they start to say things that they might wish they hadn't, I suggest a break for a cup of tea or a quick run around the block.

BEHAVIOURISM

The behaviourists regard learning as a matter of stimulus-response called 'S-R learning'. When the learner is conditioned to give the same response to a different stimulus, this is called 'classical conditioning'. If the learner is conditioned to give a different response to the same stimulus, then it is called 'operant conditioning'. Although much of the early work in this field of psychology was carried out on animals, these principles of learning are clearly useful to human beings especially in the areas of safety, good practical work and skills.

Behaviourists do not spend much time considering what processes go on inside the individual; rather they concentrate on what reaction they get to a particular stimulus. Let us have a look at two examples, one taken from classical conditioning and the other from operant conditioning and then see how they can be applied to human learning.

One of the early scientists experimenting with the process of digestion was a Russian physiologist called Pavlov. He experimented with the digestive system of dogs. Like human beings, dogs salivate at the sight and smell of food. This is not a greedy response but an important reflex. Carbohydrate digestion begins in the mouth. Pavlov called the sight and smell of food the 'unconditional stimulus' and the salivation the 'unconditioned response'. This behaviour was simple and natural. He then started to introduce a second stimulus. Every time he presented the dog with food he rang a bell. After presenting the food and the sound of the bell together on several occasions he presented the sound of the bell alone. The dog salivated. Pavlov had linked a new stimulus – the ringing of the bell – to a natural response. In this case he still called the response the 'unconditional response' but the ringing of the bell was called the 'conditioned stimulus'. This is the basic principle of classical conditioning.

ACTIVITY

Classical conditioning in human beings

When I was at school a bad-tempered teacher used to slam the door shut after he walked into the room to give us a lesson. We all jumped with a fright reaction. After a while we didn't have to hear the bang of the door, we all jumped merely at the sight of this unpopular man. If we burn our hand in a fire we jerk it backwards away from the heat as a reaction against pain. It is not long before we become conditioned to moving away from something that looks hot even before we have discovered whether it *is* hot.

Think about other natural responses which have been linked to another stimulus. Write down your examples and then turn to the notes on p.51 to see if you have got the idea.

The early work on operant conditioning was carried out on rats and other small animals. Let me give you a human example which always makes me laugh. The theory behind operant conditioning is fairly well-known. Once a large group of students were due to receive a lecture on the subject. Before the lecture began they got together and decided that they would condition the lecturer himself. It was a very large lecture theatre with a low platform in front, a lectern in the middle to hold papers and books and a radiator on either side of the stage under the side windows. The students decided to condition the lecturer to sit on the radiator on the left-hand side of the stage.

When the lecture began the students paid attention but when the lecturer moved to the right they started to yawn and shuffle their notebooks and papers. When the lecturer moved to the left they sat up eagerly and followed with their eyes with obvious interest and concentration. Throughout the lecture they continued to shape the lecturer's behaviour: to the right and they would take out a daily paper, put their feet upon the desk in front or start to chat amongst themselves; to the left and they would hang on every word the lecturer said. It took about five minutes to get him to the left and after ten minutes he sat on the left-hand radiator and stayed there until the end.

Learning, in the view of behaviourists, is encouraging the learner to have a different response to the stimulus. This new behaviour does not come about instantly but has to be 'shaped' by encouraging the change. We do this shaping all the time in social learning and interpersonal communications. I want you to like me so I smile at you. It works the other way round. I do not want you to do something so I discourage you. Physical punishment has a complex effect on human beings and is now banned from school and from the home. But every parent of young children knows that there are some 'avoidance responses' which have to be learned very quickly or the child will not survive to experience the next lesson.

ACTIVITY

Operant Conditioning and human beings
There are many occasions when we work to change the response of the learner to a given situation. All the work on assertiveness has a basis of changing an individual's response to a threatening stimulus.

Think about situations where the learner has to change his or her response to a given stimulus. Write down your answers and check the notes on p.51 to see if you agree with the comments.

HUMANISTIC PSYCHOLOGY

'The rank is but the guinea's stamp. The man's (or woman's) the gold for all that'... to misquote Robert Burns. The meaning behind this idea is to point out the importance of each individual person. You will find this underlying principle in the idea of Robin Hood, the Everyman approach to history and in many early socialist or revolutionary movements. It is an expression of support for all people rather than letting most people be treated as an inferior mass. The idea crops up throughout history and it appears in the humanistic approach to psychology.

'The best vantage point for understanding behaviour is from the internal frame of reference of the individual himself'; so wrote Carl Rogers (1951). This was an attack on the impersonal approach of the behaviourists and the clinical and rather detached Freudian psychoanalysts. As an ex-Freudian, Rogers developed his 'client-centered' therapy. He did not aim to tell you what to do but to give you the knowledge and skills to find a solution yourself.

These ideas have led to the student-centred learning approach in the theory of learning. The teacher is no longer seen as the expert who can hand down knowledge and understanding to the learner. The teacher 'facilitates' learning. The learner has first to become familiar with *how to learn* and then the teacher puts *learning experiences* in front of the learner. This approach to learning has put traditional education aside and the teacher has had to acquire new skills.

First of all each individual learner has to be considered separately. The current level of understanding has to be assessed before learning can take place. Once the baseline has been established then an action plan is worked out to achieve a particular set of performance criteria and competences. The teacher arranges coaching and practical experience which will enhance and direct this established prior

45

learning. Progress on the action plan has to be checked and adjusted by regular reviews between the teacher and learner. Finally an assessment should be carried out by a third person so that the quality of work can be appraised by a chain of assessors and verifiers to ensure the achievement of national standards.

This psychological approach to learning has had a major effect on education since Carl Rogers wrote in the 1950s. His work has also affected many other occupational areas such as health care, the law, business, management and the government.

⇨ **STOP AND REFLECT** ⇦

If you are a trained instructor or teacher do you feel qualified to teach the learner to learn, identify prior learning, make an action plan or review an individual's progress after work experience?
How long does it take you to carry out such processes?
Do you spend more time on assessment than training?

NEUROBIOLOGICAL APPROACH

This approach relates behaviour to the electrical and chemical events taking place inside the body. It is the pursuit of a scientific understanding of the activities within the brain and nervous system and their effect upon behavioural and mental processes. On the one hand science may settle the discussion about human behaviour and tell people who hold to other approaches that 'we do this because...'; on the other hand, we may not wish to know. There are some debates such as neurobiological differences between sexes or races which may not be helped by a few scientific observations in a small and specific area.

Much of science is very helpful to learning. If you know about the sensitivity of ears, eyes, noses and so on you can decide how to attract and maintain attention; if you know about brain function you can discuss channels of communication and priority on processing. All the useful knowledge about information processing within the cognitive approach is based on physiological data. Most of the advances in the scientific understanding of memory, brain processes and resulting behaviour are of direct use to the cognitive approach.

There are some scientific facts which are very reassuring to normal people. Many estimates have been made of brain capacity. It has been said that the number of possible connections in the brain are greater than the number of molecules in the universe. All those gloomy predictions that our brain cells have been decaying from the moment we were born have been refuted in some current research which suggests that brain cells can regenerate and that nerve cells can certainly grow again to give sensation to limbs which have been without sensitivity.

The suggestion that the normal human brain has an almost infinite capacity is important: it means that almost everyone is educable. Given enough time and the right opportunities, everyone can learn anything. It is a sad commentary on the training and teaching profession that so many people feel that they are incapable of learning; surely our teaching and instruction is at fault when we reject someone as a failure. How can we say they have not learned when we have used only a small part of the learner's mental capacity. *Mea culpa.*

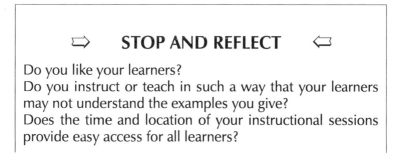

⇨ **STOP AND REFLECT** ⇦

Do you like your learners?
Do you instruct or teach in such a way that your learners may not understand the examples you give?
Does the time and location of your instructional sessions provide easy access for all learners?

Do you have a full grasp and overall understanding of your subject?
Are you up-to-date?

COGNITIVE PSYCHOLOGY

I like this approach. One of the first things teachers have to know is that they are not without personal preference. If you pretend that you can teach fairly and impartially you may give yourself away by the first subconscious non-verbal communication. I bet you can predict how your fellow teachers or instructors would vote in a general election with a fair amount of accuracy. The only way that you can present views different to your own is to admit to your learner that you have a preference and then to encourage them to make up their own minds. Read the literature and point the learner in the same direction. The teacher has no copyright on good references; knowledge is not a cake where a slice is eaten by one person and is not available to another.

These are examples of my own thoughts and this is the product of the cognitive psychological approach. Cognition is mental processes. It is all the mental processes including perception, pattern formation, working memory, long-term memory, retrieval and all the other thinking in the brain.

Let us look first at the development of cognition. Jean Piaget's (1969) thoughts are very useful here; he described different stages of cognitive development as follows.

Sensorimotor stage – from birth to about 2 years

This is the stage when babies differentiate between themselves and objects outside their bodies. Objects exist even though they are not continuously recorded by the senses. If you carry out an action, an effect occurs such as a rattle sounding when you move your hand.

Pre-operational stage – from about 2 years to 7 years

You may have difficulty in taking in the views of other people but you can grasp that words mean images or things. Objects are classified but only by single features so that something with four legs can be a 'dog', a 'cow' or a 'cat', etc.

Concrete operational stage – from 7 to 11 years

By this stage you can classify objects by several features, can think logically about objects and events but must have practical examples to understand the differences.

Formal operations stage – 11 years and upwards

You can think logically about abstract propositions and test hypotheses systematically (note the different approaches to the same questions in Figures 3.1 and 3.2). You become

TOM   DICK   HARRY

Is Dick smaller than Tom?
Is Harry bigger than Dick?
Is Harry smaller than Tom?

Figure 3.1 *Concrete operations*

concerned with the future – conceptual and ideological problems.

$$T > D > H$$

is $D < T$?

is $H > D$?

is $H < T$?

Figure 3.2 *Formal operations*

These are the developmental stages which were suggested by Piaget. Now let us try to see if they make sense for the trainer and the instructor. Although we may feel that we can ignore the first two stages because they are to do only with little children, they can have an effect on the third and fourth stages.

⇨   **STOP AND REFLECT**   ⇦

Formal operations mean the ability to use symbols instead of words. Do you understand $T > H$ as well as 'Tom is taller than Harry'?

The whole basis of an IQ assessment assumes that intelligence increases with age. Do you think that people become brighter as they grow older?

Do young children at primary school hold conceptual opinions of their own, or do they reflect the views of their teachers and parents?

Do the real clashes you have with your teenage children occur when they can use their own formal operations against your set ideas?

Cognitive psychology is a developing field and Gardner (1985) sees cognitive science as an area which draws on lots of different knowledge bases such as artificial intelligence, linguistics and anthropology as well as the more expected psychology, information processing and philosophy.

In terms of cognitive psychology, learning becomes a study of each stage of the mental process from perception to problem solving and long-term memory. This book covers most of these issues.

Notes

Classical conditioning in human beings.
You will find that human examples of classical conditioning are to do with avoidance and phobias like the example I have given or they are to do with very basic feelings of comfort and early childhood. There is nothing sophisticated about classical conditioning: it is just a simple response which becomes attached to another stimulus.

Operant conditioning and human beings.
There are many examples of human behaviour being shaped by operant conditioning. Tying a knot in your hanky is about the simplest. Much social learning is operant conditioning. You try to reinforce in other people the behaviour you wish. All assertiveness training has a behavioural basis and this can apply to every attempt you may make to 'try to do better'!

Chapter 4

Motivation and Goal Clarity

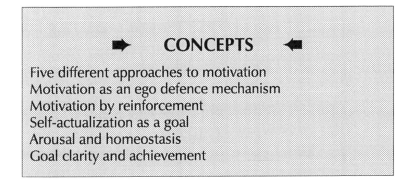

➡ **CONCEPTS** ⬅

Five different approaches to motivation
Motivation as an ego defence mechanism
Motivation by reinforcement
Self-actualization as a goal
Arousal and homeostasis
Goal clarity and achievement

FIVE DIFFERENT APPROACHES TO MOTIVATION

Promises, promises ... it is so maddening to listen to promises and declarations of good intentions when you know perfectly well that the job will not be done. There is a great gap between what people say they will do and what they actually tackle and achieve. The force which turns intentions into actions is called motivation. Some people never get started because they do not know where they are going. A clear idea of what you want to achieve is called goal clarity. So if you want to make sure that the learner learns you have to make sure that the goal is clear and the learner is motivated to achieve that goal.

So much has been written about how to motivate people that the references are very confusing. Here is a chance to see clearly how the five major psychological approaches affect the view of motivation. Motivation might be seen as:

- the defence of ego in psychoanalysis
- shaping the desired response in behaviourism
- achieving full individual potential in humanistic psychology
- levels of arousal and maintaining bodily balances
- clarifying aims; having the right attitude and problem solving.

If you have forgotten the difference between these approaches just flip back to Chapter 3 and refresh your memory. This refresher will help your long-term memory anyway – if you remember Chapter 2! Every little helps.

MOTIVATION AS AN EGO DEFENCE MECHANISM

A Freudian psychologist might see motivation as the defence of the ego against the id and the superego. There are five major defence mechanisms, outlined below.

Repression – the desire to prevent unconcious memories coming into the consciousness. This can lead to displacement behaviour. In motivation it would be the drive to follow some activity which will cut out the need to think about what really worries you.

Projection – the alleviation of anxiety and the evasion of responsibility by blaming someone else, which can lead to rationalization. In motivation this would be the excuse to cheat in an examination 'because everyone else does'.

Reaction formation – the defence mechanism which can lead you to do the opposite to what you want. In motivation this reaction may explain why some people are driven into tasks which appear to be totally unsuited to their personality and natural talents.

Fixation – the protection of an inadequate ego by remaining stuck at a particular stage of development. In motivation this may drive a person to stick with the schoolchild approach rather than move into the adult world.

Regression – the fear of inadequacy which drives towards earlier and younger patterns of behaviour. In motivation this mechanism can drive quite senior managers, for example, to behave like spoilt children.

You may find these ideas quite interesting but remember that a little knowledge is dangerous. If you want to use psychoanalysis, get qualified!

MOTIVATION BY REINFORCEMENT

To understand motivation in behavioural psychology it is necessary to look a little more carefully at the stimulus-response mechanism. Do you remember the students in the lecture on conditioning gradually shaping the behaviour of the lecturer until he was encouraged to go to the left and finally sit down on the left-hand radiator? What they were doing was rewarding him for doing what they wanted. This type of reward for the desired behaviour could be called bribery but in behavioural psychology it is called *reinforcement*.

In the classroom the teacher reinforces 'good' behaviour and 'correct' responses with smiles and nods of encouragement or even a spoken 'Well done'. This is designed to motivate school children to learn. The same expressions of congratulation please adults too. It always makes me laugh when a computer screen displays 'Well done' when I hit the correct key in a learning programme. We are all encouraged by praise and reinforcement and it does motivate us to try again. But there is one point worth raising about this sort of learning: who decides the goals?

When considering motivation, remember that in almost all formal and traditional learning the goals are set by a national board of examiners, the governors of an educational institution, a professional association or the lead body of some occupational area working with the NCVQ. The goals have been set and all anyone has to decide is whether or not he or she wants to have the paper qualifications at the end of the study.

If you want to praise your learners to encourage them to keep on trying to achieve the choosen goal then there is another part of the theory on reinforcement which will come in handy. This is the effectiveness of intermittent reinforcement.

If you always smile and encourage every piece of good work two things happen. First, it is difficult to appear genuine and false praise is very off-putting. Second, a learner gets used to the reinforcement and if you sometimes forget they stop trying and ask you why you have changed your own behaviour. The secret is to give intermittent praise. This has all the fascination of a fruit machine. On a fruit machine you keep on putting in money on the off-chance that you will hit the jackpot. If you praise your learners intermittently you will rivet their attention. Clever people have their learners working terribly hard for the most niggardly and insignificant praise.

Now we have to tackle the opposite of reinforcement. This is a real problem because there are two ways in which you can move people towards the behaviour you want:

- *punishment* – giving something that the learner dislikes, to try to cause an avoidance mechanism and prevent the learner from repeating undesired behaviour,
- *negative reinforcement* – that is, the withholding of praise and reward.

What is punishment? Punishment has to be carried out on someone who has offended against a known rule. It must be unpleasant to that person and it must be carried out by someone in authority. If any of these conditions are not fulfilled then it is not punishment but unfairness. You do not learn anything when you are punished if you do not know what you did wrong. It is not punishment if you like what happens anyway – flagellation is no punishment to a masochist. It is not punishment if your peers or an outsider knock you about; that is assault.

There are other difficulties about punishment in the learning process. Punishment is memorable; in learning it will be linked with some action or behaviour but very often the learner can't remember what the correct or desired behaviour was. They only remember the punishment, which means that the wrong response may be reinforced. It is like giving really memorable pictures of the wrong way of doing something; in learning terms this is entirely non-productive. Unfortunately, if the learner simply wants to attract attention to him or herself then punishment is an easy way to achieve that objective. We can probably remember children at school who claimed masses of attention from the teacher simply by being naughty; funnily enough they usually seemed to be the teacher's favourite which was even more rewarding for them.

Negative reinforcement seems to be much more in line with modern thinking; this is the process of withdrawing what is desired rather than inflicting what is distasteful. Bad behaviour and attention-seeking are ignored; only good behaviour and correct actions are rewarded. People who are responding well are praised and encouraged and the offender put out in the cold.

There is a danger of carrying this policy too far; you must give the non-achiever feedback on what is wrong. Feedback will be looked at more carefully in Chapter 7, but an important distinction is useful here. If you criticize a person by a comment like, 'You have made a bad job of that', you attack the person and he or she will feel the need to defend themselves. If you make a comment like, 'That is a bad job, how can we make it better?' you criticize the work, not the person, and then the learner is ready to work for improvement.

ACTIVITY

Extrinsic motivation by reinforcement
Extrinsic means coming from outside the person and intrinsic is from inside the person. All reinforcement carried out on learners to encourage them to learn is extrinsic motivation. Make a list of the forms of reinforcement which you use with learners.

> ⇨ **STOP AND REFLECT** ⇦
>
> Can you improve your techniques of reinforcement?
> Do you use punishment (this may not be physical)?
> Do you use negative reinforcement? Could you?

SELF-ACTUALIZATION AS A GOAL

The work of Abraham Maslow (1970) on motivation is very well known. Speak of motivation in training and education circles and someone will respond 'Ah! Maslow'. His ideas are useful if you take a humanistic psychological approach. The hierarchy of needs (Figure 4.1) will be described but it must be remembered that the aim is a state Maslow called 'self-actualization'. This state is the complete fulfilment of an individual's potential. The goal is very clear in this theory but the motivation lies in a rather optimistic view of human behaviour. It is assumed that all people, when free from external constraints, will work hard towards their own good and optimum development; unfortunately, some people don't. If you offer young children at school a choice, many would use this freedom to choose ignorance and not lessons. The young, allowed to choose ignorance, will never learn how to be able to be free as an adult. Many adults persist in choosing a course of self-destruction and personal ruin. Even if the theory is over-optimistic, Maslow presents a useful model which pulls together many old theories about what motivates people.

PHYSIOLOGICAL NEEDS
Food, drink, air, temperature regulation,
elimination, rest, activity and sex

SAFETY NEEDS
Protection from potentially dangerous
objects or situations. The threat is both
physical and psychological, eg fear of the unknown,
importance of routine and familiarity

LOVE AND BELONGINGNESS
Receiving and giving love, affection,
trust and acceptance. Affiliating, being
part of a group with family, friends or at work

ESTEEM NEEDS
The esteem and respect of
others and self-esteem and self-
respect; a sense of competence

COGNITIVE NEEDS
Knowledge and understanding,
curiosity, exploration, need
for meaning and predictability

AESTHETIC NEEDS
Beauty – in art and nature –
symmetry, balance, order, form

SELF-ACTUALIZATION
Realizing one's full
potential, becoming everything
one is capable of becoming

Figure 4.1 *Maslow's hierarchy of needs*

Physiological needs

Hunger, thirst or sexual desire are powerful motivating factors which encourage action. There is a danger in believing that people act in a simple way. We do not grab food from a shop if we haven't enough money to pay for it, even if we are hungry, and we do not grab a strange man or woman if we feel like a little sexual intercourse. These are sure ways to end up in jail. There is another danger in regarding such basic physiological needs as direct motivation; extreme physiological deprivation is debilitating – the starving man or woman sits down rather than stands and lies down rather than sits. Physiological needs in extreme do not lead to motivation, they produce a 'learned helplessness'. A person dying of starvation does not run about and look for food. You fight for relief supplies only if you are very hungry and not when you are starving.

A prime concern in everyday living is the satisfaction of bodily needs. These do drive people into action but the action is moderated by the customs and rules of their society. When you are teaching you will be well aware that you lose the attention of learners when the next mealtime approaches; hunger contractions and thirst distract their attention. There is also a lack of attention when stomachs are full after lunch. Much good study and learning has been carried out when the belt has been tightened and the room is cold so that sleep is discouraged. Arousal levels will be discussed in the next section.

Safety needs

People cannot operate effectively if they are constantly worried about their physical safety; you cannot instruct effectively and your learners will not study or practise if there are worries about home accommodation or security at work. The same principle applies to worries about personal health; you will find it hard to motivate a learner if either of you are worried about health or personal safety.

Psychological safety is another type of safety which can affect learning. When the learner agrees to come under your control for his or her learning you have formed a contract; you accept responsibility for the learning which will take place and your learner agrees to submit to your chosen course of action. The learner agrees to listen, pay attention and carry out the actions and activities you suggest. He or she agrees to try to answer your questions as well and as honestly as possible; this is the nature of your unwritten agreement. You must not abuse your power. You, as instructor or teacher, have no right to ask questions which are not related to the topic in hand; you must not ask about personal relationships or personal finances, for example – these are not part of the agreement. More seriously, you must not use your position to make another individual look ridiculous or lose self-respect. Not only can such an attack on another person offend the moral ethic of respect for persons but also you could create psychological insecurity which might damage future learning. We will discuss the ethics of training and assessment later on in the series. It is important to make a clear note about the damage such insecurity can do to a learner's motivation.

Love and belongingness

We are social animals. Love seems an odd thing to mention when discussing helping people to learn but it is not. Obviously you cannot love all your learners – not in the intimate sense that means a full close relationship, but you can like your learners. If you come to someone prepared to like them you will look for their good points and you will try to listen to their views. This readiness has an immediate response and the newcomer relaxes and tries hard to be equally agreeable. Carl Rogers (1970) says that a good teacher should have the following attitudes to the learner if significant learning is to take place:

- *empathy* – you should be aware of your learner's feelings and emotions; this is not the same as sympathy when you share the other's emotions, but a general awareness of how the other person feels
- *congruence* – you should be on the same level of understanding as your learner in the area of language, social experiences and so on. It does not mean that you should dress like a geriatric teenager for a young class but you should be on the same planet
- *positive regard* – you should like your learner in the way described above.

A great deal can be done for the learner in the need for belongingness. Good motivation can be generated in a group by helping everyone to learn together; take an interest in other people's progress and join in creating a group identity. It is the need for belongingness which helps to keep students attending late evening classes on dark November nights. It also helps the lone learner to want to belong to the 'club' of people who have a particular qualification.

Esteem needs

What a shame it is that only one person can win a race or come top of the class! Both are marvellously motivating experiences but unfortunately when one succeeds all the rest take a fall in incentive unless they are stout-hearted and take failure as an incentive to try harder. Normally we all need to win the acclaim of our fellow human beings.

The achievement of competence and the acknowledgement of reaching a given standard is not so exclusive as coming top. This is where fine-looking certificates, medals, plaques, cups, presentation books and so on are very motivating. The learner has the recognition of his or her peers and tutors in their success. It feels good to have such public demonstrations of achievement. The motivation does not need to be so formal. Much of the motivation to belong to clubs and organizations comes from the titles and respect that very ordinary members can gain.

It is easy to give praise where it is due in the learning situation. You can show respect for what your learners have achieved so far and flatter them by asking them for an explanation for a newcomer. In post-compulsory education this is a good tactic: you are very unlikely to have more knowledge of the subject than the sum of knowledge possessed by your group so it makes sense to use this as a resource, as well as providing motivation to the individual.

Cognitive needs

When the behaviourists started to carry out experiments on animals they were at a loss to explain why a rat in a maze didn't take the shortest route to the food every time. Lo and behold! They came up with the idea that the rat was curious and liked a change from the usual route. Man, like all other animals, is a curious creature.

There is an intrinsic satisfaction in exploration, finding meanings and solving problems; this is very useful for helping people to learn. There is also an intrinsic satisfaction in achieving a solution, like the craftsman who gets a good looking and technically well-produced object. Similarly, the mathematician or the manager likes to achieve a neat solution.

Aesthetic needs

Human beings seem to need to be surrounded by a harmony of symmetry, balance, order and form. It is difficult to say what beauty is because different people appreciate different forms of art and nature but there seems to be a universal need to avoid disorder and destruction.

This completeness and harmony can be used to motivate people to learn. It may be just the need to 'complete the set' but it is also the drive to produce something which looks right. This perception of good form and accuracy is an important driving force in the learning of all skills.

Self-actualization

When Maslow sought examples of people who had achieved their optimum potential he chose American heroes like Abraham Lincoln. Maslow's perception of the qualities and achievements of such historical figures was purely subjective – he could not have met any of them personally, and nowadays his fictional description of what he imagined these people did to achieve self-actualization seems odd. It is probably more helpful to think of what you would be like if you achieved your full potential rather than study Maslow's examples too closely.

The idea of self-actualization plays an important part in motivation for learning; all the needs we have discussed so far depend to a large extent on external or extrinsic motivation: somebody else gives the learner the prize. If you operate at your full potential you are your own critic and regulator, you have achieved autonomy and you motivate yourself – you rely on intrinsic motivation.

The state of self-actualization is the point at which the teacher has worked him or herself out of a job. Have you ever thought that you can teach someone who is potentially much cleverer and has a much greater potential for achievement than yourself? You can help someone to learn quickly and more effectively but the ultimate aim is to make yourself redundant and to launch the learner into self-regulated progress.

When you operate on your own you must have some form of regulator or you would become insufferable! I think this is where the phenomenon of 'divine discontent' comes into play. Artists may be surrounded by total praise and flattery about their work but they can be their own harshest critics; they may never be content with their efforts and drive themselves on to produce better and better efforts.

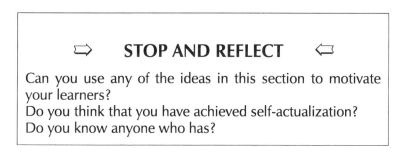

⇨ **STOP AND REFLECT** ⇦

Can you use any of the ideas in this section to motivate your learners?
Do you think that you have achieved self-actualization?
Do you know anyone who has?

AROUSAL AND HOMEOSTASIS

The arousal level is affected by thinking and cognitive processes but it is controlled by a lower part of the brain. Minute-by-minute control of the arousal level is achieved by the balance of chemicals within the body and the tone of the autonomic or involuntary nervous system.

The arousal level is important in motivating the learner. We will discuss the level of performance and the optimum arousal level in Chapter 7, but at this stage it is important to note that different learning tasks require different levels of arousal. To motivate your students to reach an understanding of a long and complex thinking problem you must keep the learners at a lowish level of arousal and be prepared for a long period of effort. If you want to motivate your students to learn something with quick hand-eye co-ordination you need to pump up the anticipation and readiness for action.

Within the body there are many self-regulating mechanisms which are given the general name 'homeostasis'. For example, complex chemical and neurological actions take place in the body but you cannot boil something up as you can in a laboratory because the body has strict and narrow limits of temperature tolerance. This means that very strict limits have to be kept on temperature control. Control of body temperature is just one of the homeostatic mechanisms.

These mechanisms use chemical and neurological methods to defend and protect the body against unacceptable change. Adrenalin and neurological adjustments prepare the body for action when a threat is perceived. This is known as the 'fight or flight' reaction. Digestion slows, skin loses capillary blood, heart rate and blood pressure increase so that everything is ready to flood more blood to the muscles if vigorous action is needed. Much research continues in this area and who knows – motivation might be a question of injecting the right chemical into the blood stream. Physiological psychology will be looked at in more depth in the second book.

GOAL CLARITY AND ACHIEVEMENT

Motivation in cognitive psychology is a question of working out what the learner wishes to achieve and setting an action plan for getting there; make sure that the learner gives this programme priority over other courses of action. We will be looking at realizing, explaining, understanding and problem solving later on but here are two theories now which fit well into the understanding of motivation in cognitive psychology.

Cognitive dissonance

This is a term which was coined by Festinger (1957) to describe a mental situation which demands a solution. If you know two things which are contradictory it is uncomfortable to try to believe that both are right. This mental discomfort pushes you to come up with a solution; it is the push for the solution which is motivational.

Suppose you smoke and you know that smoking is bad for your health. You feel uncomfortable because the two things are contradictory. Festinger would say that you were in a state of cognitive dissonance. You are pushed to come up with a solution and resolve your internal dissonance. You could give up smoking; the motivation for this action would be to resolve your internal conflict. You could say that you do not believe the case against smoking has been made and write to the papers demanding the right to smoke in theatres or on the Underground; in this case the action would still have been motivated by the drive to resolve cognitive dissonance. Motivation of this type has been used by science and technology teachers for many years to encourage learners to discover solutions to complex problems for themselves. Thinking through a problem of this type and coming up with a satisfactory answer by your own mental work produces feelings of achievement and success which are highly motivational for you!

Achievement seems to be basic to motivation in the cognitive area, and Atkinson and McClelland (1960) have done some very useful work on achievement motivation. Some people tend to anticipate and fear failure whereas others have an optimistic determination to achieve. Here are some results of general observations using these ideas:

> People with a fear of failure tackle a small task and if they succeed they say 'good luck' but if they fail they say 'bad me'. People with drive to achieve tackle the same tasks and when they succeed they say 'good me' but if they fail they say 'bad luck'.

	SUCCESS	FAILURE
FEAR OF FAILURE	Good luck	Bad me
DRIVE TO ACHIEVE	Good me	Bad luck

Figure 4.2 *Fear of failure v. expectation of success*

This fundamental difference of approach (shown in Figure 4.2) has a crucial effect on learning. Look at the general results when these two types of people tackle three different tasks.

People with fear of failure tackle:

- an easy task – they go on doing easy tasks over and over again because there is no threat. It is comforting but they are not learning anything new
- a moderately difficult task – they do not want to start and will avoid this difficult task at all costs because it might show them up. This is very bad for the learning process because by cracking problems which are just outside our experience we achieve significant learning
- a very hard task – quite against reason they may attempt this task because it has the built-in excuse of being terribly hard. But it is a waste of good learning time.

People who have confidence in achieving success tackle:

- an easy task – they often get them wrong. They don't pay attention, it is too boring and they feel that it is a waste of time. As far as learning is concerned, they are right. If you want careful and accurate work do not give it to someone who thinks the task is below them!
- a moderately difficult task – they really go for this sort of challenge. Here is something to tackle and worth trying. Lots of effective learning results from such exercises
- a very hard task – they do not attempt it. They have a clear idea of what they want to achieve and are prepared to wait until they have enough experience to tackle such a task.

This is rather a short explanation of the type of theory on motivation which is put forward by Atkinson and McClelland. It does make the point that you can motivate your learners if you place in their working memory two thoughts:

- I know what I want to achieve and
- I am quite capable of achieving it.

Chapter 5

Learning on One's Own

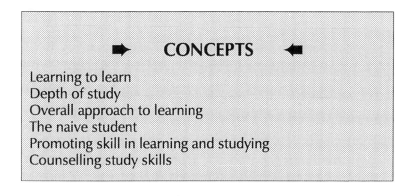

➡ **CONCEPTS** ⬅

Learning to learn
Depth of study
Overall approach to learning
The naive student
Promoting skill in learning and studying
Counselling study skills

LEARNING TO LEARN

When discovery learning was all the rage it seemed to me to be plain stupid to say to someone, 'Right, out you go, there is a field with a stream beside it, learn botany'. If learning is to be a solitary activity then the learner has to be a 'self-starter'. Normally a lot of experience, practice and above all training is required before people can manage to start learning on their own. Young students need to learn the art of learning; many adults never achieve such autonomy.

I am concerned about some recent movements in training and education. They depend heavily on an individual being able to organize work, collect material and present it in a well-documented and cross-referenced form. They demand that the learners, often young people straight out of school, are responsible for their own learning. Here are some examples:

- the equal opportunity desire to give access to learning to all
- evidence of competency achievement in portfolio form
- the accreditation of prior experiential learning
- the use of open learning resources in a local college
- study at home, in the workplace or with the Open University.

Some of my university students are a difficulty because they still need to be 'spoon-fed' in tutorials. How much more difficult it is for a 16-year-old fresh out of school or a person who has lost confidence and is coming back to study after several years at home with young children! What about people whose educational years were spent in a different system and country? What about those who managed to avoid writing much down even when they were at school? If university students still demand guidance and encouragement as well as help with study skills how can we expect the rest of the population to acquire the sophisticated abilities needed to learn on one's own?

This ability gap has to be filled by the teacher, instructor, trainer and lecturer. Unfortunately many of us trained as teachers when such skills were never considered to be necessary. You may find that the advice in this chapter, which is designed to help you to help your learner, may be useful to you as well.

DEPTH OF STUDY

There are many individual ways in which people learn and these issues, such as cognitive style and personality, are dealt with in the second book in this series. Here we examine the general way we learn. The first thing to consider is depth of study. Study can be divided into a superficial or *surface approach* and a *deep approach*.

The aim of the surface approach is to reproduce what other people said. It can be summed up like this:

- simply to reproduce part of what you have heard or read

- to accept ideas and information passively
- to concentrate only on assessment requirements
- not to reflect on purpose or strategy concerned
- to memorize facts and procedures routinely
- to ignore guiding principles or patterns.

I call this sort of thing 'popular television learning'. The aim of the TV producer is to make everyone feel an expert in half an hour. Skim the surface to catch a flavour of the topic and cram in a few facts so that you can move on to another subject quickly. The working memory and understanding are not really involved in processing the information. When you have a good grasp of a particular topic in depth and the same topic is covered on popular television, do you feel that the television was not right and that it was not like that at all? I think you are not alone. Study and understanding in depth require time, effort and internal reflection.

The deep learning approach turns other people's ideas into your own structure of knowledge. This is a process of active transformation. It can be summed up like this:

- to endeavour to understand material for oneself
- to interact vigorously and critically with content
- to relate ideas to previous knowledge and experience
- to use organizing principles to integrate ideas
- to relate evidence to conclusions
- to examine the logic of the argument.

These processes are all in line with the principles of active learning which will be discussed in experiential learning later on. Long ago the early learning psychologists talked about the acquisition and assimilation processes involved in learning. This concept is still acceptable today even if different words are used.

OVERALL APPROACH TO LEARNING

In Chapter 2 we saw how thought processes can be followed in chains of connected associations and how an overview can be taken in a mind map or logic diagram. These are the general approaches of the *serialist approach* versus the *holistic approach*.

You can study by following a series of linked and connected steps. The serialist approach can be summed up as follows:

- focus narrowly on specific learning material
- work systematically step-by-step
- look first at details and evidence
- always be cautious about accepting the interpretation offered
- enjoy tightly structured coaching and teaching
- find too many examples and illustrations distracting.

The serialist approach is the one to take if you want to go very deeply into a specific area of study; too many examples and a sweeping view of the topic are seen as a distraction because the learner wants to get to the heart of the problem.

You may wish to study in depth but not lose the overall grasp of a particular topic; to do this you need to maintain your control of how the information is selected for processing. The holistic approach puts learning strictly in the control of the learner at all times and it can be summed up as follows:

- focus broadly on a task in the context of a whole programme
- work impulsively according to mood and interest
- look first at the overall picture
- impose personal interpretation on all evidence
- prefer 'free-wheeling' coaching and teaching
- thrive on a rich supply of analogies and anecdotes.

THE NAIVE STUDENT

The clash between practitioners and academics is yet another example of two groups of people who believe they each have a monopoly of the truth. The academic will say, 'How can I assume that someone who is competent really knows the underlying principles?' The practitioner will say, 'Can that academic ever do anything in practice and get it right in the real world?' I leave out the abusive words like 'thicko', 'egghead', 'dumbo' and 'boffin'. There is nothing wrong with taking an organized approach to study; it is just the same as learning about the tools of any other skill. Although this approach is usually called 'academic' it is not to be despised for its name, just as the word 'competency' should not be despised as implying some sort of lower standard of achievement, as we will see later on.

The competent learner takes a *strategic* approach to the work of study; in this approach the learner should:

- intend to achieve the highest level of understanding
- gear work to the set learning objectives
- be aware of all performance criteria or marking schemes
- systematically work towards existing good practice
- organize time and effort to the best effect
- ensure correct study conditions and materials.

The naive student will persist in ineffectual techniques which may be a combination of prejudice, lack of study skills and the need to defend their own self-esteem. This can be summed up as:

- a rejection of academic work
- poor organization of time and effort
- poor concentration on anything but very specific interests
- low levels of motivation
- persistence in taking a surface approach.

In Chapter 4 on motivation it was suggested that people with a fear of failure avoided situations in which they might be shown up as inadequate. If you want to help students to learn effectively you will need to improve their study skills and also give them enough self-confidence to approach new topics with cheerfulness. One of the best pieces of advice I ever had as a teacher was to 'teach merrily'.

PROMOTING SKILL IN LEARNING AND STUDYING

Make sure you know what is expected from the learner

Before you start to help the learner you have to be sure that you have a clear idea of what is expected of them. So ask yourself the following questions:

- What do you expect from your learner?
- Have you made the aims and objectives clear?
- How much time do you expect them to spend in private study?
- What assessment work is required from the learner?
- Is the learner clear about how the assessment system works?

Make sure that learners know what is expected of them

You may be concerned with helping the students to learn as individuals but you must also make sure that they know the parameters of the learning game. Before you start to introduce learning skills remember the following points:

- The aims and objectives of a programme are much less clear to the students than to those who teach it.
- The majority of students are not used to handling large amounts of unstructured time for private study.
- Most learners know when an assessment is due in but have no clear plan for pacing the work to meet the deadline.
- If you concentrate too much on assignments you may reduce the overall learning on your programme.

Methods of helping with study skills

These methods can be used in conjunction with a learning programme or they can form part of free-standing coaching.

Use of the library and other learning resources

It is always very sad when learners are almost at the end of a course or programme before they realize all the resource facilities which are available in any institution. Unfortunately the traditional library visit usually takes place in the first hectic induction and there is no follow-up activity to make sure that the learners are fully aware of the services and information available in the library. Here are two activities which might help you to overcome this difficulty.

ACTIVITY

Familiarization game

The most effective form of learning is to become the question-master. Explain what you want each learner in a group to do before you send them off to the library or resources centre:

The object of this task is to help everyone to become familiar with the facilities available in the library or resource centre. You will be given a card. Your first task is to write a question on the card which can be used as a test of the ability of another member of the group to find out about the facilities. Be as inventive as you can, but you must stick to a question which highlights something useful.

You can encourage the students to set difficult questions for the others. When the learners hand back their cards you write down the answers on a master sheet and then hand back the questions to other learners to solve. This is a well-tried and usually successful game which introduces learning facilities in a memorable way, but try not to be too disruptive in the library. Of course if you are helping only one learner at a time you will have to write the question cards yourself.

What is available?

There are services which are available to help the lone learner and, again, it is maddening to find out about such facilities only at the end of the programme. Set the following task:

You are new to this institution and it would be a pity if you discovered facilities such as student services, counselling, media help, equipment, etc. towards the end of your study period. Compile a simple brochure for new students which lists the available facilities and includes opening and closing times together with the people to contact and the regulations governing the use of these services.

This task will have to be modified according to your own programme and you will have to be fully familiar with all the local facilities available. If you set the learner to find out, it helps his or her own learning – and may keep you up-to-date!

> Where is the TES
> kept in the library?

Figure 5.1 *Library game card*

Pamphlets on study skills

These are often sent out to learners before the course or programme starts. Here is an example on 'Taking notes':

- Listen carefully and question (mentally) the points that the speaker makes.
- Remember that the idea is to summarize and not to take down dictation.
- Listen for the words which indicate the pattern of the presentation, eg, the headings or sub-headings.
- Look for the signal words which stress important points eg, 'next', 'above all'.
- Get definitions down word for word.
- Note opinions and differentiate these from facts.
- Don't be afraid to ask the speaker to repeat a point. If you cannot see or hear, say so.
- Keep your notes in a loose-leaf file so that you can add to them later.
- Review your notes as soon as possible after taking them. Correct anything that is unclear, expand a topic where relevant and check the spelling of technical words.

ACTIVITY

Why not write down your own list of simple instructions to help your learner to make, record and organize notes?

Workshops on study skills

There are many different ways in which you can help your students to acquire study skills. You can give them sound and well-tried methods, you can recommend strategies, you can encourage them to help themselves, you can isolate new skills which may be required on your course or you can target those who are having particular difficulty. Here are some quick notes on examples of these approaches.

Recording notes
Give a mock lecture to a group. Encourage the learners to discuss their notes in pairs. Finally have a plenary session to recap on what you actually said and give some clear hints for more effective recording.

Recommend a systematic approach to reading
Take a specific system like 'SQ3R' (Atkinson *et al.*, 1993) which stands for:

Survey – scan the article and get an overview.
Question – by asking what you know about the topic, what you expect to be told and what you expect to learn.
Read – with the active intention of being able to answer the questions you have just raised.
Recall – what you have read.
Review – from the text what you may have left out.

Learning-to-learn workshop
This may start with a text which the students are asked to read on their own for meaning and content.

Then work follows for the students in pairs to get a quick check on what they have learned and what they are trying to do.

The pairs are then asked to work individually to try to get greater meaning from the text.

After this stage the students work first in pairs, then in fours and finally in a group to share their common experience and to check on their understanding of the text.

Study strategies
These concentrate on the different aspects of skills which are needed for study. These might be:

● how to write down notes for recall

- thinking skills
- summarizing and and forming images to create memorable associations
- elaborating, which is the process of connecting your existing knowledge and experience to the new knowledge.

COUNSELLING STUDY SKILLS

You may be able to encourage the learner by explaining what they will achieve at the end of your programme. The learner may acquire new skills as part of your programme, which may have value. These new skills may help the learner when they try to gain employment.

⇨ **STOP AND REFLECT** ⇦

List the skills which may be ancillary to your course of study. Do you think that you need to give special training to help your students complete the work successfully?

Can you sell your course by pointing out that the students will gain commercially-useful skills?

Your learner may have special learning difficulties. Little extra training has been given to instructors and teachers in spite of policies which integrate those with special learning difficulties into general training and teaching. If you are to help people with special learning needs to be successful then special instructing and teaching techniques are involved.

Look at the general ways in which you can enable people to learn. What are the real barriers to learning for a particular learner? What extra facilities might be needed? These facilities may be physical or psychological. You should find that there is specialist advice locally available to help those with learning difficulties.

When you have removed the barriers to learning for those with special learning difficulties, you can move forward to teach and instruct in the usual way. This is an important basic principle to remember. If you start to treat learners with physical or psychological barriers to learning as different from other learners then you run the risk of being patronizing or distorting your normal teaching relationship. If you treat learners with physical or psychological barriers to learning as normal learners with a particular barrier that you both have to overcome together, then no distortion occurs in the teacher-student relationship.

Many learners do not like to admit that they may have a learning problem, especially not to the teachers who are likely to mark their work. There have been some sad cases recently where able students have opted out of study or even committed suicide when they felt that they had no one to talk to about learning problems.

Where would your student go if he or she wanted to talk to a neutral person? You might want to think about a separate time or place where your learner can talk in private about their own current difficulties. This might simply be a question of not hurrying away too quickly after work. For years I have tried to calculate how much time I spend on 'corridor tutorials'!

What do you think a tutor should bear in mind when encouraging a nervous student to seek help? I think it is a good idea to go back to the work of Carl Rogers, with his recommendations that the teacher should have empathy, congruence and positive regard. If you really care, then lots of potential problems with communication fall away.

I will end this chapter with a brief account of the historical origins of self-instructional techniques. We owe a great deal to the classic paper, 'Goodbye, Teacher' by Keller (1974). This system of programmed learning, developed in the armed forces, came to be know as the 'Keller plan'. Keller (1974) summarized the five main features as:

- The 'go-at-your-own-pace' feature which permits the student to move through the course at a speed commensurate with his or her ability and other demands upon his or her time.

- The unit perfection requirement for advance, which lets the student go ahead with new material only after demonstrating mastery of that which preceded it.
- The use of lectures and demonstrations as vehicles of motivation rather than sources of critical information.
- The related stress upon the written word in teacher-student communication.
- The use of proctors which permits repeated testing, immediate scoring, almost unavoidable tutoring and a marked enhancement of the personal-social aspect of the educational process.

Chapter 6

The Role of Language in Learning

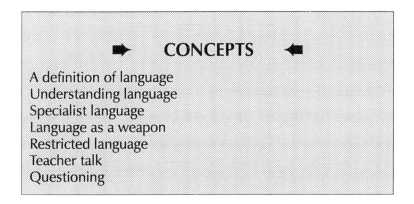

➡ **CONCEPTS** ⬅

A definition of language
Understanding language
Specialist language
Language as a weapon
Restricted language
Teacher talk
Questioning

A DEFINITION OF LANGUAGE

I am sailing across Falmouth Bay to the Helford river. It is evening. The sun which has been golden yellow all day is turning a rich golden red as it falls in a pale apple green sky. The blue-green sea now fades to subtle patches of dark green and purple. The bright yellow sands under the cliff are drifting into honey-coloured edging. The white gannet turned soft pink by the setting sun takes one more perpendicular drop into the darkening sea...

A better writer than I would use a cleverer combination of words to describe colour but there is no way anyone can describe every subtle shade of the continuous spectrum. We have to use known words like red, orange or yellow which have an agreed English meaning and then we add extra words like 'rich', 'pale' and 'honey' to try to increase the spread a little, but we never get near the full range of the spectrum because it is infinite.

Provided that we have no colour-blindness we can all use the cones in our eye to detect all shades. Descriptions of colour use words which lump together bands of light wavelength, brightness and tone. This description has an agreed meaning to everyone who speaks English. Words are vital for communication and thought but it cannot be assumed that we all understand the same meaning of a particular word. Do we, for example, all mean the same thing when we talk about 'justice', 'democracy', 'truth' or even 'football' or a 'holiday'?

Language and words, together with a wider range of special symbols, are essential for helping people to learn. They play a special part in learning a skill, learning from experience, thinking, memory and all the other cognitive processes.

Brown, a student at Harvard University, once wrote in an unpublished MA dissertation, 'We use words as symbols which denote both concrete objects – such as houses – and abstract ideas – like justice'. He formulated three rules to define language:

> Words must mean the same things to all speakers of the language.

> It must be possible to communicate about the past and the future as well as the present.

> A limited number of sounds and signs must combine to make effectively an unlimited number of messages.

UNDERSTANDING LANGUAGE

What kind of knowledge do we need to understand language? Here is a list of the basic characteristics of any language and its use:

- the letters of an alphabet
- the sound of each letter, called phonemes
- the sound of combined letters like 'er', called morphenes
- what words mean, ie, lexical knowledge

- the combination of words and sentences in the correct way, ie, syntax
- the understanding of the meaning of words, ie, semantics.

It is not enough to study only these aspects of language. You would also have to learn phonetics and the rules of pronunciation. If you have used one language since birth much of this knowledge will have been acquired in childhood. Sadly for instructors, teachers, trainers and learners alike we cannot assume that everyone can speak and write correct English. The expression 'every teacher is a teacher of English' is not true in my experience.

In an excellent book called *How to Write and Prepare Training Materials* (1991), Nancy Stimson helps adults to brush up their understanding of written English. She has a chapter on punctuation which gives excellent examples of current usage. The section on grammar reminds us of what we may have forgotten from our schooldays. The spell check on your personal computer cannot be relied upon to sort out the differences between, say, *principle* meaning an important rule or guideline and *principal* meaning the head of an institution. Nancy Stimson has a section about spelling in her book which clears up many such common confusions.

SPECIALIST LANGUAGE

When I was teaching in India I learnt a great deal, not least that there are many different perspectives. The Western approach to philosophy and education theory is certainly not the only one. Words within a language are developed to express new concepts and ideas; if some ideas are not part of a particular culture then the words to express these concepts are not developed within the language. At present English is a grand language for discussing technology and science because English speakers have been the first to describe advances in so many developing technologies.

I put this to a colleague who supported the theory in rather a charming way. I asked him how many languages he spoke and he replied that he had three. I asked him what they were. He replied, 'I use English language for my work as an engineer and I teach, read and study in English. I use Hindi for politics. You can really get into a wonderful heated argument when you use Hindi. I make love in Bengali'.

Normally we do not have to learn a new language for our ordinary instruction, but we do have to introduce specialist language when dealing with a specialist subject. Technical and work terms have specific and essential meanings within a trade, craft or profession; often the use of the correct terminology is taken as a sign of competence in a specific field. Use the right words and you may enter an exclusive club which might consist of lawyers, motor vehicle engineers, physiotherapists or football fans. Specialist language is in part a vocational skill.

Some instructors put each new term onto a piece of card and ask students to place the new words on the appropriate parts of machinery with spot magnets. This is a useful technique for learning the names of parts of a lathe or an industrial sewing machine. I scored maximum attention in a pre-nursing class by getting a fit second-row forward rugby player to strip off and let the students write the names of his muscles on his skin. There are many other ways of making new terms memorable.

One of the problems is converting commonly-used names into the correct specialist terms. You can try a gradual change over to the specialist terms in the following way. Suppose you want to introduce the terms 'oxy- and deoxyhaemoglobin':

- start off by explaining that dirty blood is carried to the lungs, where it is placed in contact with oxygen. The waste product is removed and cleaned blood is now ready for recirculation round the body
- then explain that dirty blood is carrying deoxyhaemoglobin
- the next time turn the expressions round so you say blood carrying deoxyhaemoglobin would be called dirty blood
- finally, the description begins to shape up to 'deoxy-haemoglobin is carried to the lungs where the CO_2 is transferred and oxy-haemoglobin is the ready for recirculation'.

The widespread habit of abbreviation is a real menace. I was at an assessor's meeting the other day and someone mentioned 'NCR'. Now what, I thought to myself, have cash registers to do with this meeting? I asked what 'NCR' meant. I was told that it was a pad of forms which produced two or three copies if you pressed firmly enough on the top sheet; the initials stood for 'No Carbon Required'. I felt an idiot asking such a simple question until half of the other people at the meeting admitted that they didn't know what NCR meant either. You can have fun by asking what SOB stands for and then announcing that it is used in nursing to denote 'Shortage Of Breath'!

The instructor must be satisfied that every learner is familiar with any of the initials which are used in their new subject. Not knowing the meaning or substituting another meaning for initials is one of the quickest ways to cause confusion. You must make certain that you and your group all start from the same agreed understanding of the words and expressions used.

LANGUAGE AS A WEAPON

The trainer, teacher or any other instructor must realize that when learners submit themselves to a learning discipline they have the right to expect respect. Language is the primary vehicle for conveying this respect and mutual politeness. If the teacher can build up an atmosphere of polite and kindly verbal communication in the class then the student will build up confidence to try out new ideas. Once this is established in the class, effective learning will follow; it is a question of creating psychological safety for the student.

Physical punishment has almost entirely disappeared from all learning processes nowadays. The new-comer to learning at work, in a training or educational establishment is not beaten for shortcomings. Words and disparaging non-verbal communications can be much more devastating. A recent television programme on a harsh penal corrective institution in the USA showed that no physical violence was used by the guards. Prisoners were not allowed to look at the warders but the warders were allowed to stare in that most threatening animal way directly into the faces of the prisoners. All other discipline was imposed by verbal threats, sarcasm and abuse. It was a terrifying regime.

Sometimes teachers are not aware of the devastating effect their own words can have on a learner. Words can make a person want to curl up and die, especially if they are designed to belittle the learner in front of his or her peers. I do not suggest that you don't use language, both verbal and non-verbal, to control the learning process but I do suggest that you should be fully aware of the powerful weapons you are using.

RESTRICTED LANGUAGE

Basil Bernstein (1971) described two types of language code: an elaborate and a restricted way of using language, which is a helpful distinction when considering language and learning.

The *elaborate* code is open to all speakers of English. Free of slang, abbreviations and contrived words it is often called 'BBC English' or 'received English'. Typically spoken in formal situations, it can be understood fully by anyone who can speak English. Nowadays it is rather more fashionable to champion regional accents, local dialects and non-standard forms of English; in the interests of encouraging equal opportunities in a multicultural society there is pressure to accept all different forms of spoken and written English. Variations from standard form can only be used in teaching when everyone can understand the meaning. Because there will be times when the group is heterogeneous all teachers must be able to give an explicit explanation which any other English speaker can understand.

The *restricted* code depends on the use of 'in' terms, abbreviations, slang, specialist language and any other form of communication known only to a restricted group. The outsider does not understand what is going on and the communication within the group can become very stylized. The use of thieves' cant and the development of rhyming slang are examples of a restricted code. The code can often depend on non-verbal communications and can become a complete sign language. Tick-tack men wearing white gloves pass information about betting odds at a race track without saying a word. This restricted form is not used for simple matters; listen to people bidding in a game of bridge, working at the stock exchange or discussing a complex business transaction. Communications between people of like knowledge and interests don't have to be made explicit on every point. Sentences do not have to be completed and much time can be saved by nods, grunts, single words or phrases and a lot of time is then available for thinking about the real matter in hand.

I have used a restricted code to build up the confidence and psychological safety of the learning group. Many older students have had poor experiences and suffer a poor self-image after school. It is possible for the teacher to use a restricted language to build up a 'gang' class which you can then develop into a group geared to success in learning. Using Carl Rogers' principles of congruence, empathy and positive regard you can build a successful group image in which everyone has a feeling that it is safe to try and learn.

⇨ **STOP AND REFLECT** ⇦

Can you build up a rapport with a class by using 'in' jokes and phrases to bind the group together?
Do you feel that you have empathy with the group through a shared language?

TEACHER TALK

Many methods have been developed to measure the type of verbal interaction which is taking place in the learning situation. Here is one simple method developed by Ned Flanders (1970) which is a useful way of separating out simple interactions that will help you to understand the nature of language in a one-to-one or group situation.

Flanders's interaction analysis

The system is designed to record typical interactions between teacher and learners for a short time during a session. Each number represents a common type of interaction. Before you can record a session you have to learn the list of numbers and interactions. The observer writes down a number every time there is a change in interaction; if the same type of interaction continues the same number is recorded every 20 seconds. It is not difficult to become a trained observer because the number of different interactions is restricted to ten. The numbers and types of interaction are as follows:

1. *Physical conditions.* When the teacher is talking about the physical conditions of the learners, by asking if they are too warm or too cold for example, then a 1 is recorded. This interaction may be about seating, need for food or drink and any other area which affects the learner's physical well-being.
2. *Teacher encouragement.* A 2 is recorded for any interaction in which the teacher praises, congratulates, or acknowledges the worth of a learner's contribution to the group. This is an interaction where positive reinforcement takes place.
3. *Using a student's own suggestions and ideas.* When the teacher picks up the learner's own ideas and uses the suggestion or idea to continue with the interaction, this is recorded as a 3.
4. *Teacher asks questions.* An easy interaction to recognize: if the teacher asks a question, record a 4.
5. *Teacher talk.* This is usually the most common interaction of all – most teachers will not shut up! When the teacher is simply talking, record a 5 and go on putting down a 5 every 20 seconds as long as the monologue continues.
6. *Teacher instructing.* This type of interaction differentiates normal teacher chat from directions and instructions. Identify this interaction with a 6. It will reveal a lot about the nature of the interaction when you analyse the session.
7. *Teacher disapproving.* The 7 is used for an interaction when the teacher is correcting, being sarcastic or rebuk-

ing a student. Group discipline has to be maintained and this interaction records such moments.

8. *Learner replying to teacher's direct question.* This interaction comes into play in traditional question-and-answer techniques. The teacher asks a question and the student replies to the teacher – a clear example of an 8 interaction.

9. *Learner puts in his or her own ideas.* The number 9 represents an interaction when the learner puts forward his or her own ideas. It may follow a formal interaction which has been given an 8 or it may be general group discussion where one learner responds to another learner's suggestion.

10. *Silence or confusion.* There may be several occasions when everybody is silent because there is a pause for thought and consideration. In this situation a 10 is recorded. Sometimes everyone talks at once and the interaction is confused; if this is the case, a 10 is recorded.

These numbers are not mathematical numbers representing quantity or quality; they represent what is going on at a particular time. Here are a couple of imaginary examples.

Example 1

Suppose we have a sticky class with a tired and cross teacher trying to get some work out of frustrated students. The teacher starts off by talking and the observer would record 5 every 20 seconds. Then teacher throws in a question – 4 – silence follows – 10 – a longer silence – another 10. The teacher starts to get cross – 'Come on you lazybones, I've only just told you that' – 7 – the teacher gives a few instructions and the observer records a 6 and perhaps another 6. The teacher asks another question – 4 – and a student gives a tentative reply – 8. The teacher cannot resist a bit of sarcasm – 7 – and the class relapses into dejected silence so the observer records a 10 and another 10.

Example 2

A good and jolly interaction is taking place with learners chipping in with enthusiasm. 1 – the teacher is making sure the group is comfortable, 5 – the teacher says what is going to happen next, 4 – the teacher asks a question to get started, 8 – a learner replies quickly, 9 – the learner starts to expand on his or her answer, 10 – confusion as everyone wants to join in, 2 – the teacher praises the class for their enthusiasm, 3 – the teacher picks up the learner's idea, 4 – the teacher asks another question to set things off again and (lots of 9s) the learners hold a lively discussion.

ACTIVITY

Using Flanders's interaction analysis
First learn the categories one to ten. Then use these categories to observe the verbal interaction which is going on in someone else's class. Alternatively, tape record sections of your own class and 'Flanderize' it afterwards.

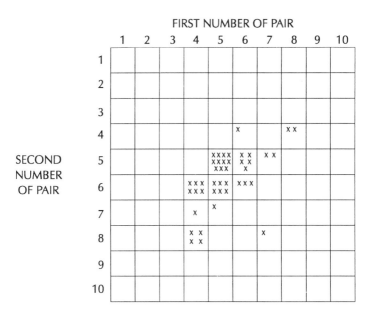

Figure 6.1   *Flanders's analysis of when teacher is being bossy!*

You will find the amount of time that the teacher is talking is rather daunting; if the teacher talks for half the time in a one-hour lesson and there are 20 learners in the class, that leaves just one and a half minutes for each student, provided you allocate the talking time evenly between learners. This seldom occurs. What usually happens is that one or two talkative learners monopolize the rest of the time. This is where you begin to ask yourself about small group methods, some of the learning strategies which are the topic of the third book in the series.

QUESTIONING

This section is concerned only with the general link between language and questioning as a technique for monitoring learning; other aspects of questioning will be dealt with elsewhere. Let us look at some general points which can be made about questioning and answers.

Do not waste time with questions unless they serve a recognized part of delivery or encourage people to learn. There are times when I would like to climb inside the students' heads so that I can have a quick check on what they know and to rewire a few connections! The best you can do is to ask 'indicator questions'. You can write these into your lesson plans. They are the type of questions which require only a short sharp answer but which indicate very quickly whether learners have or have not 'got the hang of it'.

Go back to the example of introducing the idea of oxy- and deoxyhaemoglobin with the starting point of a general phrase, 'dirty blood'. If you ask the question, 'Which is the only artery in the body to carry deoxygenated blood?' you can check very quickly if they have got the idea. If the answer comes back, 'the pulmonary artery' then you know that they have grasped the whole concept of double circulation in the body.

It is unfair to expect students to come up with the exact words we have in mind even though we do need to know how much the students have learnt. One of the most painful lesson experiences is to watch a teacher who has the answer, framed in a particular word or phrase, firmly fixed in his or her head. This is the only answer which the teacher will accept. The poor students, who may be anxious to please, rack their brains to come up with the required term. They may bomb the target with many near misses but never achieve a direct hit. Disappointment for the teacher and great loss of face for the students results. This is, of course, a stupid situation. There is no way that a teacher can track the thoughts of a whole class of students so closely that the exact phrase is triggered in every head; to expect the precise answer and no other is to court disaster.

Consider the question, 'How many times does two go into four?' The teacher and many in the class may expect the answer 'Two times' but 'every time' is just as good. By insisting on narrow and rigid answers the teacher may stifle invention and creative ideas.

ACTIVITY

Writing good questions

Indicator questions are hard to write because they have to encapsulate a summary of what should have been learned. They must not require long tedious answers but rely on a trigger response to give you the green light to go ahead.

Try some in your next lesson plan and then record how they work. You may need to do some sub-editing because they are rather like writing advertising copy. It is very difficult to be accurate and succinct.

Chapter 7

Learning a Skill

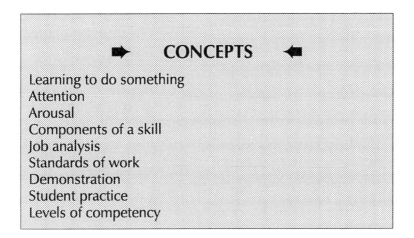

➡ **CONCEPTS** ⬅

Learning to do something
Attention
Arousal
Components of a skill
Job analysis
Standards of work
Demonstration
Student practice
Levels of competency

LEARNING TO DO SOMETHING

There is a difference between learning how to do something and the process of learning from activities and personal experience. The process of active learning and work experience is called 'experiential learning'. This type of learning method is the subject of Chapter 8. In this chapter we are looking at how people acquire skills, which is learning to do something to a high level of performance. If you watch someone carrying out a skill the performance appears to be:

fast
easy
smooth
confident
unhurried
efficient – with no wasted movements
effective – with no surprises
automatic – requiring little effort
consistent – maintaining high standards.

ATTENTION

You can probably add to this list of characteristics of a skilled performance but you would be unlikely to put in 'pays attention'. Most people carrying out a skill do not seem to concentrate on the job in hand at all. Indeed, it may appear to be the very opposite. People shave, put on make-up, hold a conversation, tune the radio, make a telephone call, even gesture and swear at passing motorists when they are driving with no apparent difficulty at all, but the question of attention in practical skills is of the greatest importance. Accident reports clearly show that if the cause is human error the major factor is loss of attention or failure to pay attention.

Selective attention

The link between a skill and attention is the process of selective attention. Suppose you write down all the sensations you are experiencing at the present moment both from outside your body and from inside. 'It is a very warm and humid day in June. I am feeling hot. My shoes are sticking to my feet and my arms are a bit prickly. The chair is hard and too low so my long legs are under tension' and so on. You should be able to see how many complex inputs are competing for your attention. Did your list include physical sensations and internal thoughts?

Now try another exercise. Select one of the inputs and concentrate upon it. Once you do this all the other aspects should be pushed out of your attention. By the process of selective attention a person is able to pull one recording sense or chain of thought into direct focus at the expense of all others.

Importance

Another feature of attention is the ability to select what is really important. The cocktail party phenomenon has been mentioned already but here is a reminder.

Suppose you are at a busy party – drinking cocktails or not – and you are chatting away to a friend when someone, a little distance away, mentions your name or your home town or your favourite subject or someone you know. You hear this and immediately tune into the selected conversation. You may have to listen over competition from several other conversations but it is relatively easy to eavesdrop when something is of particular interest.

This demonstrates our ability to home in on one sensation and exclude the stimuli. What happens to the other stimuli? This cocktail party effect shows that the non-attended stimuli are lost if not needed. Our attention mechanism selects what is important to us. When you are doing two things at once, what are the types of incident that make you suddenly change and select only one? You will probably find that this focusing comes down to one of two things: a physically arresting or novel stimulus, or something which is of biological importance to you. In other words, your attention is switched by sudden surprises or by any matter which is important to your health, well-being or safety.

Mental processing

Attention when performing a skill can either be a *serial* or a *parallel* process within the brain.

Serial processing is paying attention to one stimulus after another. Some suggest that this is the only way to progess because you are less likely to make mistakes if you pay full attention to the job in hand.

Parallel processing relies on carrying out two jobs at the same time; in this case one job is a semi-automatic and well-learned task and the other is something which can be dropped quickly when an emergency occurs in the semi-automatic task.

Capacity is an interesting factor which arises during parallel processing. Suppose you are driving a car and chatting to your passenger at the same time. When an emergency arises such as a car appearing on your side of the road or a large patch of deep water ahead, you stop chatting and concentrate completely on your driving. You might voice your concern but your mind is concentrating on the task of driving.

Vigilance

Finally let us look at *sustained attention and vigilance*. It is of vital importance that warning signs are noticed quickly. This is like the lookout scanning the horizon from the crow's nest. The life-threatening change may be only a small smudge on a murky horizon or, in the case of modern control systems, a small bleep on a computer screen. Unless the controller or watcher maintains a high level of attention the first warning signs are likely to be missed.

Because we know that our attention is most likely to be attracted if the change is sudden, vivid or vitally important to us, feedback systems need to be geared to our attention mechanisms; human beings are poor constant watchers. Computers, on the other hand, are infallible in this area. If computers are used to give immediate feedback to the human observer the person can maintain attention at a more effective level.

It is interesting to see how the relationship between the person and the computer has changed to produce the optimum performance by using the best assets of each:

the computer – the reliable recorder
the human – the innovative problem-solver.

On the flight deck of a modern aeroplane or at any major control panel the selection of important incoming information is of the utmost importance. Much skills training goes into the recognition of what is important. The trouble for human beings comes when things remain the same for so long that our normal level of vigilance begins to fall and we start to lack attention. This is why electronic engineers work so hard to produce effective alarm and warning systems and why arousal is important in a skilled performance.

AROUSAL

It is not very difficult to measure the human level of arousal or excitement. One way is to measure the sweat in the palm of the hand, which increases as the individual becomes more excited. I have experimented by placing two electrodes on a learner's hand, connecting up a recorder for electrical conductivity and then picking a quarrel. A steep increase in conductivity is quickly seen on the recorder, especially if the student is of a choleric nature. This is a simple way of demonstrating arousal. There are more sophisticated ways which do not interfere with carrying out physical work.

Figure 7.1 is an optimum performance diagram showing the way in which performance efficiency varies with the level of arousal. It can be seen from this diagram that there is an optimum level of efficiency. This will vary with the type of performance or skill. When carrying out, or learning to carry out, a complex and delicate operation you need a low level of arousal which can be maintained over a sustained period of time. You will have seen horse riders steady themselves before attempting a series of complex and high jumps in the showjumping ring. The same riders will 'psych' themselves up before the headlong dash of the cross-country. If you want to carry out a task which demands a high level of body and eye coordination then you need to have a high level of arousal. Another good example of this is the way in which field competitors in athletics often get the crowd to cheer and clap in time to raise the general feeling of tension.

Individuals may find their performance enhanced or inhibited by an audience; some people are deliberate sensa-

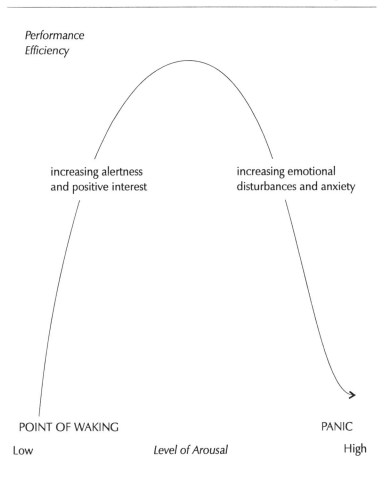

Figure 7.1 *Optimum performance*

tion-seekers. We will consider personality and individual differences in the second book in this series.

COMPONENTS OF A SKILL

All skills have three components. Whether it is the skill of an eye surgeon, a bricklayer, an actor, a pastry cook, a hotel receptionist, a design engineer, an interviewer, a health professional or any other occupation, you should find that each skill contains the following three elements.

Psycho-motor skill

In all skills, however cerebral, there is some body movement. Part of a skill is the movement of some part of the body and in very active skills, like ballet dancing, these manual parts are highly complex and controlled.

Perceptual skills

All skills are controlled, practised, precise and accurate. They require very sophisticated control mechanisms which are carried out by the senses. The maker of things has to judge length, angle and texture. The negotiator or the musician has to listen for tell-tale changes in tone of speech or in note. All the cues for action and the checks for correct performance need trained perceptual skills.

Cognitive skills

Every subject, occupation or process has a language which may consist of words or symbols, and the skilled person has to understand and operate in that language. Plans, patterns, codes, symbols and technical words are all used within problem-solving and the operation of a skill. There are thinking and memory aspects to the skill which may be numbers for distance in carpentry or notes in music or psychological terms in personnel management.

ACTIVITY

Recognizing the components of a skill
Pick a few skills and try to list the three aspects of each one under the headings of *psycho-motor*, *perceptual* and *cognitive*. You might identify the language being used in the underpinning knowledge of the skill.

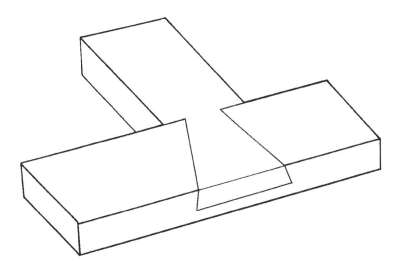

Figure 7.2 *Skill perception*

JOB ANALYSIS

Before you can learn to perform a skill and, more importantly, before you can teach it, you have to analyse the job. The difference between simply doing a job and telling someone else how to do a job can be seen in the following activity.

ACTIVITY

Describing a skill
Write down the steps you would use to screw the top on to a jar of honey.

There is a gap between what we think we do and what is really necessary for the task. This gap causes problems in written instructions and manuals. Good teachers of skills make sure that they analyse the whole job before starting to teach the individual skills that are required to complete the task.

First it is necessary to break down the skill into a list of smaller jobs or operations, then each operation has to be broken down into a series of detailed steps. It is important to make sure you don't miss out any vital steps; however there is a danger of going too far in this breaking-down process. Usually it is foolish and time-consuming to go into details of separate eye and hand movements; such detailed movements need to be analysed only in very complex manual tasks.

When you have analysed the psycho-motor skill aspects of the job then cover the perceptual and cognitive aspects. These are identified as *key points*. There are usually four parts to the key points which need to be written down in detail when analysing a skill. You should have notes on:

underpinning knowledge
the main cues for each stage of the process
fault recognition and rectification
safety rules.

Reasons for particular operations

No skill is mindless. The essential underpinning knowledge has to be identified and known by the skilled person. Sometimes this underpinning knowledge may be detailed and need a lot of theoretical support and in other cases it may be simply of the 'because it's there' type. This is important in all basic skill teaching and, as we shall see, it is becoming a special problem in NVQs at the higher levels.

The main cues

Although many different types of learning come into skills learning there is a strong link with behaviourism and operant conditioning. The analysis of a skill includes the recognition of the stimuli which trigger the next response in a skill; analysis can be treated as a chain of stimulus-response mechanisms. You have to identify the main cues which form the framework for the skill.

How to rectify mistakes

When learning a skill, the recognition and identification of the cause of errors is most important. You must know when something is wrong. The teacher should write down what is expected at each stage so that the learner can correct any error immediately; this is where the perceptual skills and the cognitive skills work hand-in-hand. Successful plans for learning a skill contain progress descriptions of what a product should look like or what should be happening at each stage in a process; hints and tips for rectifying errors are placed in the learning materials alongside each main cue.

Safety rules

Safe practice is not an optional extra. No teacher or trainer should ever demonstrate or use unsafe practice. 'Do as I do' is the only approach to skills training. It is bad enough if a trained teacher uses poor overhead transparencies and scribbled handouts (especially if the teacher is a trainer of teachers!) but it is criminal to use dangerous techniques. Make sure that you are fully familiar with the current regulations which apply to your skill area and be meticulous in using the correct procedure and the careful preparation of materials. This is the best way to help your students to learn correct practice. You may be an 'old hand' but you have the responsibility for shaping the practice which will last the student for his or her working career.

Before we move on to an activity which should help you to sort out the four main sections of job analysis, let us look at stimulus and response within a skill which is based on behaviourism and operant conditioning.

So far we have concentrated on one stimulus giving rise to one response. Learning in this system is putting a different and desired response to the stimulus. There are chains of stimuli and responses in psycho-motor skills so that the response to the first stimulus becomes the stimulus for the second response. A skilled performance has closed loops of stimulus-response chains where the cue or stimulus for one action results in a response which becomes the cue or stimulus for the next action.

Many quick hand-eye coordination skills are of this type. Take the action of gear changing in a manual gearbox at speed, a golf swing, a smooth keyboard performance or the fast chopping of a vegetable. In these skills there is no time for cognitive adjustment between each action of the sequence. The smooth performance is a simple, behaviourist chain of stimulus and response. These aspects of a skill are called a *closed loop*.

The overall aspect of the skill is an *open loop*. The skilled performer chooses when to change gear, which club and which swing are needed for a particular lie of the ball, which piano piece to play, which piece of typing or when the onion needs to be added to a dish.

Decisions have to be made as to which actions are appropriate in the open loop of a skill; this is a case of detective work. You have to get the right response to the cues as they arise during performance. Cue recognition needs perceptual skills and cognitive skills again. The skills trainer should make a list of the main cues which need to be recognized because they change the progress of the skilled performance and trigger off the closed loops of trained psycho-motor skills.

 **ACTIVITY**

Identifying key points
Take a skill, or a small section of a skill, and work out

- the reasons for each operation
- the main cues
- how to rectify mistakes
- the safety rules.

STANDARDS OF WORK

There are *standards* in any skill which have to be identified, recognized and achieved. The learner must be aware of what is expected. This is goal clarity which is essential to motivation. For years there has been the idea that any work done by a student is acceptable because it represents his or her own creative ideas; the idea stems from a laudable wish to avoid stunting the free expression of the individual. This approach questions the right of the teacher to impose authoritarian ideas of quality; I am convinced that this attitude is a mistaken interpretation of freedom and equality. Ultimately the instructor causes serious harm to the learner if poor standards and quality of work are accepted. It is only by striving towards excellence and high standards that the skilled person will reach independence and that special feeling of pride and satisfaction in a job well done. All competency-based qualifications are very useful in this area because they lay down clearly what the learner is expected to be able to do, under which conditions and to what standards.

⇨ **STOP AND REFLECT** ⇦

Do you think that the learner should be encouraged to produce their own work without reference to arbitrary standards?

Do you think that students like to be told where they stand in relation to set criteria?

Do you think that the teacher can encourage by praising individual work and make clear the standards that will be acceptable in competition within the workplace?

There are three standards that are relevant to any skill.

Standards of preparation

All skills need to be stage-managed. The correct tools have to be assembled, the room has to be arranged with chairs and lighting, surgical instruments have to be set out or kitchen ovens have to be heated up. There are a hundred and one ways in which the performance environment has to be prepared and checked. The list of key points is useful as a guide to this preparation. The learner must be able to make proper preparation. Such activities must be included in any assessment or marking plan.

Standards for the process

There is the correct or preferred way of carrying out a skill which has to be learned. For example, there are ways to approach a potential client in business, ways to hold the scissors when cutting hair and correct ways to saw, plane or file. All this must be laid down and taught; there are correct sequences and the timing of each stage is important. If you are learning the skill of producing hamburgers there is no commercial sense in making one hamburger every half-an-hour if you want a skill which will get you a job in a fast-food restaurant.

Standards for the product

When you are planning to teach a skill it is most important that you consider how you will help the student to recognize a suitable standard for the finished product. 'Is it the right size?' 'What are the tolerances?', or simply, 'Does it look right?', 'Does it feel right?', 'Does it smell right?' This is the essence of skills and good craftmanship.

Finally you have to define the *conditions* under which the skill will be carried out. So many skills are related to employment that it is worth considering where these skills are going to be performed; if the programme of study is related to employment, then it should take place in conditions which are nearest to the real work situation.

When I am discussing the idea of the conditions under which the learner will work I sometimes use the example of my husband and the skill of tying a bowline. A bowline is the knot used by sailors for a safety line or any situation requiring a very secure knot. He was taught by the Royal Navy to tie a bowline underwater, in the dark, upside-down and so on. This skill is extremely useful when sailing, especially if the conditions are difficult, because he can retie a stormjib sheet in the middle of a gale in the Bay of Biscay or refix a topsail halyard when closing a lee shore without any difficulty at all.

ACTIVITY

Standards and conditions

Make brief notes on the standards required for a skill in your area and divide into:

- standards of preparation
- standards of process
- standards of product
- conditions.

DEMONSTRATION

Demonstration reveals interesting differences in the ability of individual teachers to coordinate speech and action. It is a test of their ability to parallel process. Some people cannot talk and concentrate on a good performance; some can talk beautifully and carry out a poor, fault-ridden manual performance; some can use words and non-verbal communications simultaneously and with the ease that creates a superb display of action and commentary. A really good talk through skilled demonstration is a joy to see and experience; if you look at some stage performances you can see examples of excellent demonstrations. We will study the techniques and strategy of demonstration in the third book in this series, but for now it's worth noting a few important points.

Make sure that everyone has a clear view of the demonstration

This is essential stage management. Before the demonstration make sure that everyone can see by arranging chairs, using a mirror to show the hand movements the right way round or to give an overview if that is appropriate. If the demonstration involves the use of small tools, use a video or a micro-projector. In a crude way you can silhouette small tools and artifacts on the overhead projector which makes a quick enlargement for the class.

Prepare stages of the process

Everyone is familiar with the TV cook who, halfway through the preparation of a dish, whips out a previously completed example to show the final product. The phrase '...and here is one that I made earlier' is now a cliché. Better prepare several examples of the work at various stages of completion. I have seen excellent demonstrations of clothing seams, welding, hairdressing and even accountancy illustrated this way.

Match the words to the actions

You will have to practise before the demonstration. It is a universal teacher skill, like explaining, which can be acquired by practice. I usually practise in the bath where I feel safe and uninhibited.

STUDENT PRACTICE

The use of *modelling* has long been included in learning a skill and is usually called 'Sitting by Nellie'. It is a popular technique and is still very useful so long as the model is carrying out the approved practice correctly.

Learning from instruction sheets

I mentioned before, under the components of a skill, that it is very difficult to put down all the stages in a skilled performance, but it is a skill which the instructor must acquire.

Part-practice for students

A lot of research has been done on the best method of learning parts so that the whole can be mastered; the schedule of parts for practice is chosen to suit a particular skill.

Practice of the whole and the importance of feedback

Some parts of a skill – the closed loop in quick manual skills, for example – must be practised as a whole. (The significance of these issues and the so-called plateaux of learning are discussed in the third book in this series.) The idea of levels of skill attainment is important to understanding competency learning. A short summary forms the last section of this chapter.

LEVELS OF COMPETENCY

Think about car drivers and their ability to perform separate tasks while they drive. Most people can drive an average family car reasonably safely under normal weather conditions. These people may have some difficulty parking in a busy town street and they may be hopeless on black ice but by and large they are competent under normal conditions. Now think of a British Metropolitan Police driver who has undergone an advanced driving course. This driver is more than competent. He or she can cope with very bad weather and road conditions and their car-handling skills are well above those of the average motorist. Rally drivers are in a different league again. You could call them master drivers.

There are undoubtedly several more levels of driving skill but these three examples will be enough to make the point. In driving we have identified:

- *Competence* – the skill level of the average driver
- *Proficiency* – the skill level of the trained police driver

● *Mastery* – the formula one driver.

When helping a learner to achieve a skill it is very important that the instructor and the learner have a clear idea of which level of competency is the target. Our study of motivation makes it clear that well-defined goals help the learner. The difficulty for the instructor comes when he or she has to recognize that while the learner may achieve mastery the teacher may not; in practice the teacher may be too old or too untalented to achieve such a high standard of performance. A lot can be done in coaching by giving feedback and advice but in the end the teacher or instructor may have to bow out with dignity. Already we have talked about the ultimate aim of teaching as making yourself redundant; here is another example. You can, as a teacher or trainer, console yourself with the fact that the world is full of younger and less-experienced learners eager to acquire your skills.

Chapter 8

Experiential Learning

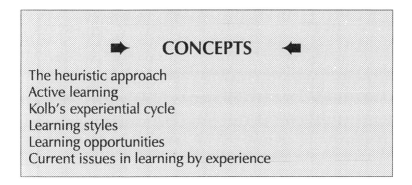

➡ **CONCEPTS** ⬅

The heuristic approach
Active learning
Kolb's experiential cycle
Learning styles
Learning opportunities
Current issues in learning by experience

THE HEURISTIC APPROACH

Sometimes it seems there is nothing new in education and training. The ideas keep going round in circles. Certainly the idea of learning by doing has been with us a long time; fashionable in the mid-nineteenth century, it reappeared in the mid-1950s as 'Nuffield Science'. At that time the Nuffield Science Foundation set out to reform science education in schools, through understanding science by practical work and discovery learning. It was an ambitious plan and the method was usually highly effective but very expensive in time, materials and teacher hours. The long-term effect was not to create alternative science courses in schools but to shake up all practical science work throughout the school system. At this time learning by doing was called the 'heuristic approach' and it was summed up as:

I see – I forget
I hear – I remember
I do – I understand

Let us clarify again the difference between learning to do something and learning by doing. Learning a skill is acquiring the knowledge, perception and physical movements to be able to carry out a skilled performance. Learning by doing is a common teaching and learning method: 'active learning' is an essential part of student-centred learning, work-based learning, competency-based learning and experiential learning.

Because the activities are largely student-based and monitored by the teacher or trainer, this type of learning seems to be dominated by checklists and 'a list of useful things to do'! In this chapter I will set up the area under discussion and then, as an 'activity', I will ask you to write a checklist of important factors. I have written what the experts suggest immediately after each activity so that you can check your own list, but remember that your checklists may be the best basis for you to use in practical instruction: the expert lists are only a guide to make sure that you have not forgotten an important point.

ACTIVE LEARNING

When the student is actively involved with the learning process there is a shift of emphasis away from traditional teaching methods. There are several advantages.

Attention

Active learning helps to solve the problem of maintaining attention. Remember the principle:

My holiday snaps are always more interesting than yours.

By taking an active part in the process of learning, the student stops being a passive observer and has something to do. All inactive observers have periods of short 'micro-sleep' when their selective attention wanders away to other incoming stimuli. Physical activity keeps up the student's level of arousal and interest.

Long term memory

If the learner has a personal stake in learning then there is a built-in assurance of greater effort and interest. In the discussion of memory and learning on one's own, we saw how the learner has to wrestle with new material. This effort results in a sense of personal ownership of the new knowledge.

Motivation

Active learning means that the students are responsible for their own learning. Thus the student must be a willing partner in the learning process; the instructor or teacher does not have to drag unwilling students through education or training.

Individual attention

Active learning means that each person has to participate in the process and so the teaching has to cater for individual needs. This has the advantage of the humanistic approach to learning with concentration on the needs of each learner.

The movement towards active learning and the subsequent student-centred learning has meant a fundamental shift in the skills which are required by the teacher and the instructor. Traditionally the teacher is an expert in a particular subject area and is taught techniques of putting over information, demonstration and formal assessment. The instructor or teacher in the system of active learning becomes the *facilitator* of learning. The student is encouraged to *learn how to learn* and then a set of learning experiences are arranged to meet that individual's needs.

The new learning process requires teacher skills of counselling, planning, review, managing experiences and types of assessment which were unknown a few years ago. Let us work through the process of experiential learning and then review the implications for the instructor or teacher at the end of the chapter.

KOLB'S EXPERIENTIAL CYCLE

In 1984 D A Kolb published a book called *Experiential Learning – Experience as the source of learning and development.* In it he described a four-stage model of learning by doing. This was a rather complex cyclical model so a simplified version is given in Figure 8.1 as a useful starting point.

I will work round this cycle to reveal the significance for the teacher and the learner but first here is a list of the main points of experiential learning that Kolb considered to be important:

- the learner is involved in *the active exploration of the experience*
- *the learner must reflect* on their experience in a critical, selective way
- learners must be committed to the *process of exploring and learning*
- there must be scope for the learner to achieve some *independence* from the teacher
- the teacher imposes some *structure* on the learning process so that the learners are not left to discover by random chance.

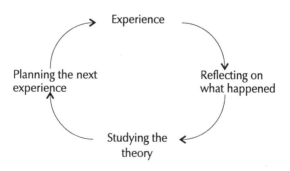

Figure 8.1 *Simplified Kolb's cycle*

- *exposure to experience* is necessary for the learner
- the learner must feel safe and supported so that they are encouraged to *value their own experience*
- experiential learning follows a linked cycle so the teacher or trainer must provide *appropriate learning activities and teaching methods* to support each stage.

Stage 1. Planning the next experience

This involves the preparation of the learner so that they make the most of their experiences. The method used may be either action planning or writing a learning contract.

ACTIVITY

Action planning

What do you think are the essential principles of action planning? Try to make a short list and then check the ideas put forward by Kolb.

- Writing an *action plan* may be as simple as jotting down a set of things to do or the instructor using a standardized form laid down by a validating body. Theoretically the purpose of an action plan is to clarify the aim of the learning experience.
- It is helpful to the concept of learner independence if learners are encouraged to *set their own objectives* for inclusion in the action plan; this is a good way of highlighting the important features of learning. Such statements as 'After this I will be able to...' are very useful when it comes to reflecting on the effectiveness of the experience.
- An important stage in planning is to choose the *type of experience* which should go into the action plan. It may be carrying out a survey or project, designing an experiment, or undertaking some work experience.
- Assessment and evaluation have to be planned right at the beginning. If *observer checklists* are needed they

should be designed as part of the preparation. Sometimes such checklists are provided by a validating body but even so it is a good idea to encourage the learner to look at and carry out preparation for assessment. Very often learners will be required to produce and present their own evidence of the successful completion of the learning experience and it is helpful to encourage responsibility for learning early on.

● *Learning contracts* need special attention.

ACTIVITY

Learning contracts
Try to list the tasks required in writing learning contracts and then check against the suggestions put forward by Knowles.

The list of tasks suggested by M S Knowles (1990) is useful; here are the main points:

● Diagnose your learning needs
● Specify your learning objectives
● Specify learning resources and strategies
● Specify evidence of accomplishment
● Specify how the evidence will be validated
● Review your contract
● Carry out the contract
● Evaluate your learning.

Stage 2. Increasing awareness of experience

The learner needs skills to make the most of opportunities, so priming of what to expect makes a very big difference to the worth of the experience. It is rather like a naive person in a picture gallery, where the only differentiation possible is 'I like that' and 'I don't like that'; once that decision has been made the visit becomes boring. However, a trained observer can offer an opinion on many aspects of the painting – composition, colour, texture, content, craftsmanship and so on. To the expert observer the picture gallery is of endless fascination and he or she is never bored.

ACTIVITY

Skills needed to get the best from experience
List the skills which you think are needed to prepare the learner to get the best from an experience and then compare your answers with the suggestions below.

- The learners are encouraged to carry out as much *preparatory research* as possible; formal study of the underpinning knowledge is helpful in enriching the experience. He or she will be in a position to make intelligent and useful observations which will result in significant learning. If you have a sound understanding of the nature of the topic, you recognize what you are seeing and new experiences and information will be stored available for future use.
- *Preparation is useful for writing a record or a log book.* Notes taken at the time of the experience are much more useful than relying on recall – remember the limited capacity of short-term memory. The learner with a prepared format at the beginning can keep a more detailed and accurate record.
- *Observational skills* can be improved. We have seen that sketching is one way to sharpen up visual perception. (The techniques of visual learning will be discussed in the third book in this series.)
- *Listening,* and all other *interpersonal skills,* are essential in this type of learning method. I suppose this is one answer to the charge that there is a difference between training and education. All training these days depends heavily on the learning of interpersonal skills and communication skills. That must be sound education.
- Above all the skill which a learner must master, if he or she is to benefit from experiential learning, is the *ability to formulate a question.* Questioners can give themselves

115

away so easily by irrelevant, ill-considered or just plain silly questions. The expert or professional takes an adverse view of the questioner immediately and cuts down any further effort to help.

Stage 3. Reviewing and reflecting upon experience

This is the most difficult stage. Does everyone learn from experience? What do they learn? You do not learn much about surgery by undergoing a major operation but you might learn a great deal about interpersonal skills by watching trained health professionals at work. There is another difficulty about reflection: in practice it favours those with linguistic skills. The same problem occurs in accreditation of prior learning. Students may have learned a great deal from an experience but unless they can articulate their experiences and write these reflections down in clear words they are not accredited with having learned anything.

ACTIVITY

Techniques for helping learners to reflect on their experience
List the ways in which you would encourage the learner to reflect on experience and then look at the suggestions below.

- *Log books and diaries* are a useful way of reflecting upon what you have learned. This method is especially useful for 'woolly' experiences like social skills in the health profession. Being able to write down actions and feelings in clear language can be a legitimate part of learning because it is essential to communicate with others in the same field.
- *Video and audio tapes* for an immediate reminder of what happened have two uses. First, they act as a memory aid and we have seen that repetition aids recall. Second,

they help get over a serious problem with learning from experience. If you are in the middle of things, your attention cannot be focused all the time on what is best for learning; you tend to get involved, so that selective attention starts to work and you may miss some essential point of the experience. When you have the chance to see the events again you have a much better chance to balance and select from the learning.

- You can use *peer appraisal* which has the added advantage of helping everyone in the group to learn to become more aware of the learning which is taking place and generally improves the group motivation by encouraging all participants to play an active role in the learning process. However, all groups have to be trained in the techniques of peer appraisal because the naive assessor may fall into the trap of giving too much negative criticism or overstepping the limits of the assessor's role. We will look at this method in the fourth book in the series, where we will see that it can be useful to learning but there must be no drift into amateur psychoanalysis.

- Sharing your experiences with a group in *structured discussion* is a good method of helping you to understand by reflecting on your experiences. It is surprising how talking aloud can clarify the picture of what has happened to you. I am sure that discussing the day's events when you get home is a splendid aid to learning and memory.

- *Debriefing* can be much more formalized and formal debriefing should always be arranged when a group of learners undergoes such activities as work experience. Formal debriefing is also essential when the learners become involved with a lively role play. You simply must not send people out into the street without first making sure that they have come firmly back to reality.

━━━━━ **ACTIVITY** ━━━━━

Debriefing
Make a checklist for debriefing and then compare this with the suggestions from Gibbs.

Gibbs (1988) wrote a debriefing plan to be applied after the initial experience. You guide the learner through the following stages:

- Write down a description
- Write down feelings and emotions
- What was good and bad about the experience?
- Analyse what was really going on
- Write general conclusions
- Write specific conclusions
- Make personal action plans for next steps.

Stage 4. Studying the theory

This stage is the one which is so frequently left out of the programme when experiential learning is being used. There must be a time when the appraisal of a learning experience is turned into theoretical application and abstract ideas. Much recent criticism has focused on the lack of depth in these student-centred approaches to learning. Some of the programmes are all about testing and not about the development of sound theoretical underpinning. It is important that the theory is consolidated before moving on to the next stage of the experiential learning cycle.

- I feel there is room here for a *formal input* of theory and theoretical study. You might point the learner in the direction of the library and resources centre. (We will discuss this methodology in the third book in the series.)
- There may be room for *formal testing*. At present examinations are out of fashion in some quarters but I think that people are beginning to appreciate some of the advantages of checking, from time to time, what learners can recall, provided that the testing is carried out

with reliable, valid questions and in a user-friendly style. I have found that learners find it very comforting to know that they do know some things well; it is also helpful for a learner to recognize and identify that which needs more thought and study.

⇨ **STOP AND REFLECT** ⇦

Do you think that appropriate testing can be helpful to a learner?
Do you think that continuous assessment can confuse a learner?

LEARNING STYLES

Honey and Mumford (1992) carried out work on Kolb's experiential learning cycle and developed a theory about preferred learning styles. They produced a set of 80 questions which indicate preferences for active, reflective, theoretical or pragmatic learning. Here are some examples of those questions:

- The 'Activist' would reply 'Yes' to the following:
    - I prefer to respond to events on a spontaneous, flexible basis rather than plan things out in advance.
    - When things go wrong I am happy to shrug it off and put it down to experience.
    - I enjoy the drama and excitement of a crisis situation.
- The 'Reflector' would reply 'Yes' to the following:
    - I like the sort of work where I have time to 'leave no stone unturned'.
    - I think that decisions based on a thorough analysis of all the information are sounder than those based on intuition.
    - On balance I do the listening rather than the talking.
- The 'Theorist' would reply 'Yes' to the following:
    - I have strong beliefs about what is right and wrong, good and bad.

     – I find it difficult to come up with wild, 'off the top of my head' ideas.
     – I steer clear of subjective and ambiguous topics.
- The 'Pragmatist' would reply 'Yes' to the following:
  - I have a reputation for having a no-nonsense, 'call a spade a spade' style.
  - At meetings I put forward practical, realistic ideas.
  - I do whatever is expedient to get the job done.

When the questionnaire is completed, the total scores are added up; each learning style area can score up to 20 points. A 'thumbnail' sketch of the type of person who fits into the different learning styles is then linked to the learning activity which this 'type' enjoys or dislikes. The learning style theory fits into the Kolb cycle, as shown in Figure 8.2.

In practice I have found that this theory is very popular with the young. The 16- to 18-year-old students from all types of subject learning seem pleased to find out whether they are activists, reflectors or theorists. Few of them seem to be pragmatists. Many find comfort in the theory and use it as an excuse for not getting on well at school!

With older groups there is a tendency to score quite highly on most, if not all, of the styles and the questionnaire seems to be rather more indicative of personality measurement than learning styles. I have come to the conclusion that an experienced, mature learner can use all styles and select the appropriate style for any particular learning situation.

Figure 8.2 *Learning styles and a simple learning cycle*

⇒ **STOP AND REFLECT** ⇐

Do you think you have a preferred learning style?

Do you think it is linked to your personality or with your self-image?

Do you think you can help your students to learn in all styles so that they can complete the full Kolb's cycle easily?

Would you change your teaching approach if you felt you had a large number of, say, activists in your group?

Do you think that some subject areas give advantage to people with a particular learning style?

LEARNING OPPORTUNITIES

This combination of Kolb's theory and Honey and Mumford's ideas of learning styles has been developed into some very useful suggestions for work experience (see Figure 8.3).

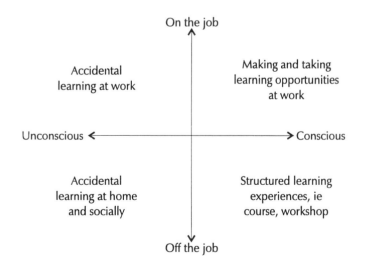

Figure 8.3 *Opportunities for learning on and off the job*

Honey and Mumford (1992) combined their earlier theory of learning styles with the theory of experiential learning to come up with the idea of using learning opportunities to develop personal effectiveness. They recommend that people at work or on work experience become learning opportunists. There are many potential benefits:

- adding an interesting extra 'learning' dimension to all you do
- making learning from experience a more conscious and deliberate process
- making one more purposeful; determined to extract learning even from unremarkable, routine events
- helping to learn from successes not just from mistakes
- using a variety of opportunities:
  - *situations within the organization*: meetings, familiar tasks, unfamiliar tasks, task forces, customer visits, visits to plant, visits to the office, managing changes, social occasions, foreign travel, acquisitions, closing down something
  - *situations outside the organization:* voluntary organizations, domestic life, industry committees, professional meetings, sports clubs
  - *processes:* coaching, counselling, listening, modelling, problem-solving, observing, questioning, reading, negotiating, selling, mentoring, public speaking, reviewing, auditing, clarifying responsibilities, walking the floor, visioning, strategic planning, diagnosing problems, decision making
  - *people:* bosses, mentors, network contacts, peers, consultants, subordinates, people who write learning workbooks
- making it more likely that one will transfer learning from a specific situation to a broad range of other situations
- meaning one can articulate what has been learned and communicate it to others
- providing a recipe for continuous improvement and for helping others to improve
- helping one to keep ahead of, and attuned to, change.

Once you take the attitude that every event and personal experience can generate reflection and self-appraisal then all experiences take on a new value and each one can be seen as beneficial. Carl Rogers' theory was: don't waste time on self-recrimination, embarrassment or shame but get on with optimistic learning and self-development. This attitude spreads into all aspects of your life. You have only a relatively short working life and so you might as well make the most of every minute of each day. Optimistic learning is one of the best ways of improving personal effectiveness.

The attitude of learning opportunism makes it possible to view all experiences as a potential area for useful learning.

CURRENT ISSUES IN LEARNING BY EXPERIENCE

The amount of time it takes

There is no doubt that active learning takes much longer than the traditional process of simply 'Telling 'em and thumping it in'. The formation of groups, the briefing for the action, the debriefing and then discussion and reflection take a lot of time.

One of the main reasons why Nuffield Science was not more widely adopted in the 1950s and 1960s was the time and effort required in preparation. The current move for competency-based learning is producing the same problems. Any teacher can say what has to be done; a verbal description does not take long. But it is quite a different matter when the teacher has to do something. The science-based, technology and skills teachers are well aware how long practical work can take but other teachers in less practical subject areas have to find out for themselves just how long active learning can take.

Getting the timing right

Activities are only the first part of active learning. It is easy to finish the active part of the learning session with too little time for the learners to reflect on what they have done, and the whole effect is lost if you say, 'Well we will sum up next week...'. Each active session has to be consolidated immediately. As a general rule you will need at least the same time for reflection and assimilation as you do for the activity. This time for consolidation of learning may even run into subsequent sessions and can be increased to twice or even three times if the topic is an essential fundamental principle.

Helping the learner cope with the responsibility

Can your learners compile, write up and produce well-structured and well-produced records of active learning? These are sophisticated learning skills. You may find, as I do, that the teacher has to do some fairly basic work on learning techniques before the students can benefit from an experiential approach.

There is a well-circulated myth that adults like to be responsible for their own learning. The teacher or instructor 'need not worry about deadlines' because these mature and responsible older learners will get all their work in on time. With the exception of a few, highly autonomous and delightfully mature human beings, I don't think that this is so. It is very difficult to be a complete 'self-starter' in learning. You might feel that your learners need help with:

- timetables
- deadlines
- checklists
- criteria
- portfolio preparation
- record-keeping
- reflection schedules
- assignment organization and
- presentation techniques.

Chapter 9

Understanding and Thinking

➡ CONCEPTS ⬅

Insight
Reasoning
Explaining
Barriers to understanding
Understanding
Thinking
Practical thinking
Meta-cognitive skills

INSIGHT

Do you remember that in Chapter 1 we discussed perceptual constancy? Look it up if you have forgotten. We talked about Gestalt and the way we tend to look for grouping, continuity and a complete pattern when receiving new information. While we take in information from outside our bodies we are constantly searching this information for meaning. It is easier to accept new information if it is meaningful. This is the 'chunking' in short-term memory. We want to lump things together so that we can say, 'Ah! Got it!' or, 'That's something I've seen before'. These and similar expressions are a signal of the relief we feel when we recognize something familiar. Sudden insight is very like any other sudden relief of tension – we relax, the tension flows away and, above all, we feel good.

The trouble with insight is that it may be based on the wrong information. We can all jump to the wrong conclusion; we can experience the well-being of having had a feeling of understanding but be mistaken. We can reach an unsatisfactory conclusion when we do not have enough information or we have not done enough thinking about the evidence. There is an old expression, 'consistency is the virtue of fools'. I find it particularly irritating when I am battling with a problem and expressing what I believe is reasonable doubt to find myself confronted with the self-satisfied smugness of someone with a facile but wrong solution. The rigid adherence to a wrong conclusion which arises through ignorance and lack of thought is called 'functional fixedness' and it is a great barrier to successful problem-solving.

There are some factors which inhibit realization. We will look at these in the second book in the series but it is worth noting here that understanding may be inhibited by personal factors:

- some people are not open to new experiences
- some people follow habit and are unwilling to follow intuitive hunches and new ideas
- sometimes a person's own reasoning gets in the way. This sounds odd but the individual's reasoning may be defective and so he or she rejects new ideas by inadequate thinking and illogical reasoning.

REASONING

The rate at which we think and reason varies from one person to another; moreover the rate at which any one person thinks and reasons may vary from one occasion to another.

Accepting negative information is a much slower process than accepting positive information. For example, it is harder to comprehend:

> If the circle is *not* brown, then the triangle is *not* green

than it is to grasp

> If the circle is red then the triangle is blue.

Thinking and reasoning take even longer because you cannot assume that your learner follows strict logic; they may lack thinking skills.

Concepts are the tools of reasoning. Reasoning depends on concept formation. Just as we found that memory classifies pieces of information into clumps so that the memorizing process is easier, we store factual knowledge in classifications which we call concepts, which makes the handling of information easier. These concepts can be of solid material objects or they can be ideas.

Try the concept of 'table'. Think of all the tables you have seen and try to decide on the essentials which something must possess to be correctly referred to as a table. We cannot say that it has four legs because some tables have three legs and some have a single pedestal. You might refer to a flat surface, to something at roughly waist-height or to something at which we can sit. But we are still in difficulty as coffee tables are low and, if anything, we tend to sit on them and not at them. However, we all agree about what is meant by a table and freely use the concept in our reasoning.

Let us look at a more complex example. Try the reasoning behind the concept 'bachelor'. Even though I have a science degree I would not be called a bachelor because I am female. My three grandsons are not called bachelors because they are all under seven and not old enough to father children. My son, who has recently been divorced, would not be called a bachelor because he was once married. So we can see that reason demands we use the concept of a bachelor normally if the person is male, mature and unmarried.

We reason within a set system. This system is sometimes called a 'schema'; because we are dealing with human beings there can be many schema. Here are four descriptions of some general frameworks within which we might choose to reason:

- seen as a play containing information about the characters, setting and script
- seen as theory to give meaning to what is happening around us
- seen as a computer system to process the information we receive
- seen as a digestive process which reduces everything to small, simple parts.

EXPLAINING

There are three general ways of explaining:

- interpretive
- descriptive
- reason-giving.

The *interpretive* approach explains what is happening. These explanations specify the central meaning of a term or statement or they clarify the use – like 'What is a novel?'

The *descriptive* explanation describes processes, structures and procedures such as 'How does a bicycle pump work?'

The *reason-giving* explanation involves principles or generalizations, motives, obligations or values. In general it may also give causes, but most philosophers like to make a distinction between reasons and causes.

ACTIVITY

Three different ways of explaining the same thing
Think about your teaching and pick out something that you have to explain very often. Now try to write down three separate explanations which represent what is happening overall, what is happening in detail and the reason why it is happening.

Above all you should realize that even though students have a responsibility to pay attention and to listen, the explainer has the responsibility of making the work interesting and clear. The teacher should be prepared to explain in different ways so that students who failed to grasp the first explanation may find the second fits more easily into their internal schema.

BARRIERS TO UNDERSTANDING

You may not know the meaning of the word which is being used

This can be a real problem – it may be a completely new word which you have never heard before. There is a double disadvantage because not only do you pause in your attention to puzzle about the meaning but, because you have interrupted the flow of thought, you have not recorded what was said after the word.

Another barrier to understanding may be that a specialist is using a common word for a very special meaning within the subject. A lot of the trouble in understanding law, sociology and economic principles, for example, falls into this category. Words which we use in everyday life have a defined and special meaning within the subject.

There can be different meanings of the same word

This is an extension of the specialist meaning idea. Some words have several totally different meanings and the understanding of the meaning depends on the context. When introducing a new word you will often find your learners giving a suprisingly diverse set of meanings to that word simply because they have very different backgrounds and experience. For example, I had difficulty in my first degree course because the lecturer talked about 'corn' as a source of carbohydrates. To some people 'corn' means maize but to a northener like me, 'corn' is a collective word for cereals – barley, wheat and oats.

There can be a misunderstanding of English grammar

English is a complex language. The complexity brings a subtlety and delicacy of meaning which greatly enriches our lives, but this same complexity can be a barrier to the understanding of what is being said. I did some very cheerful team-teaching once with a pedantic, theoretically sound science teacher called Leo. He would state the clear scientific position and I would follow with an informal interruption: 'What this really means is...'. It is surprising how often my task was one of sorting out his English construction and not the scientific principles.

There can be misunderstanding because of context

Guy Claxton (1988) gives a splendid example of context affecting understanding:

ACTIVITY

What is the context?
Read the following passage and then turn to the notes on p.138 to see if you have recognized what was being described:

With hocked gems financing him our hero bravely defies all scornful laughter that tried to prevent his scheme. Your eyes deceive he had said: an egg not a table correctly typifies this unexplored planet. Now, three sturdy sisters sought proof forging along sometimes through vast calmness yet more often over turbulent peaks and valleys. Days became weeks as many doubters spread fearful rumours about the edge. At last from nowhere welcome winged creatures appeared signifying a momentous success.

Early work on this type of lack of understanding when you know the context was illustrated by Bransford and Johnson (1973). In this example they used a picture as an 'advanced organizer'.

ACTIVITY

A picture as an advanced organizer

In this example, read the following passage first. Then look at the picture in the notes on p.139 and re-read the passage. Do you understand better when you have a pictorial organizer?

If the balloon popped the sound wouldn't be able to carry since everything would be too far away from the correct floor. A closed window would also prevent the sound from carrying, since most of the buildings tend to be well insulated. Since the whole operation depends on a steady flow of electricity, a break in the middle of the wire would also cause problems. Of course the fellow could shout, but the human voice is not loud enough to carry that far. An additional problem is that a string could break on the instrument. Then there would be no accompaniment to the message. It is clear that the best solution would involve less distance. Then there would be fewer potential problems. With face to face contact, the least number of things could go wrong.

Sometimes you do not understand the inference

Within a group you can have 'in-talk' which is incomprehensible to the outsider, like the 'thieves' cant' which we talked about in Chapter 6. If you are not part of the group you are excluded from understanding.

A very old example can be used at a family dinner when there are guests present. As the dishes go round the table you might say, 'FHB', which means that there isn't enough for everyone to have a portion; 'FHB' is an invitation to leave everything to the guests: 'Family Holds Back'.

I use another example which comes from a wartime story about an escape, called *The Wooden Horse*. If the prisoners wanted to warn others that their conversation was being overheard by the guards, they used to say, 'Goon in the block', which meant that one of their German guards was within hearing range. Nowadays, if my family telephone when I have someone listening at my end, I simply have to say 'Goon in the block' to excuse any lack of familiarity and any unwillingness to talk on my part.

Personal but erroneous explanations

Recent work on the understanding of science has shown that some teaching leaves the school children more confused than they were without science lessons. The research is well-documented and is difficult for serving teachers to accept! The explanation seems to be that everyone has naive theories about most basic scientific principles and we hold onto these ideas tenaciously because many scientific explanations don't seen to make sense. If school children hear science explanations and still remain convinced about their own natural theories, then great confusion is caused.

Current research suggests that the best way to overcome this problem is to begin by asking the school child how they explain a particular scientific event. The naive explanation then forms the basis of experiment, and the scientific principle is accepted on practical evidence and the older self-made theory is rejected.

UNDERSTANDING

The process of understanding usually involves one in making a comparison. The new information or the study of existing knowledge has to be put into some form of value system. There are six possible processes:

- judgement
- measurement
- contrast
- relationship
- quality
- value.

When trying to understand, you may ask yourself, 'How is this information the same (or different) from ideas that I already have?' Then you could move into one of the six ways of making a comparison.

We will consider problem-solving in Chapter 10, but it is worth mentioning now that the next stage is classic search questions which ask:

- what
- who
- how
- why
- where
- when
- which.

THINKING

Go back to Chapter 3 and look again at the five separate psychological approaches. Of these we have already defined learning and motivation; now let us examine thinking.

Thinking from the Freudian perspective

Freud suggested that thinking arises from trying to satisfy some fundamental urge of the id or superego. These internal demands cause images to form in the mind. The needs have to be satisfied and thinking then becomes part of the problem-solving exercise to achieve satisfaction of the demands.

Thinking in behaviourist terms

Behaviourism is concerned with linking stimulus to response. In the section on skills learning we saw how 'chaining' of S-R takes place. In this approach to psychology, thinking is a process of association. This is a very old view of thinking, first formulated in the 17th century by John Locke. He proposed that one idea led to another. Thoughts were made up of chains of ideas and new thoughts, together with learning, occurred when we made additions to these chains. Nowadays this idea would use word association as an example.

Thinking as adaptation to the environment

Jean Piaget (1952), the developmental psychologist, put forward the view that thinking arises from a continuing process of adaptation to our environment. Human infants build up a model of the world from their experience and this forms the schema or frameworks which we all use. New experiences are measured against our frameworks of past experience and we think about what to do. Each new experience is then recorded and integrated into the schemata.

Thinking in humanist terms

The Russian psychologist, Vygotskii (1962), argued that thinking arose from the personal need to restructure situations cognitively, commonly called 'figuring it out'. He argued that a child can see that things are not the same and needs to work out how to cause change in the environment. This is why Vygotskii put such an emphasis on the importance of language in the development of thinking.

Thinking as a cognitive process

We have already discussed in the section on 'cognitive dissonance' thinking as resolving discrepancies. Dewey (1952) put forward the idea that thinking arises when what we expect does not quite match up to our expectations. He suggested that most of the time we act automatically. It is only when something unexpected occurs that we ask ourselves, 'Now why did that happen...?'

PRACTICAL THINKING

'The main difficulty of thinking is confusion' says Edward de Bono (1986) in his book, *Six Thinking Hats*. He suggests that we try to do too much when we think. Emotions, information, logic, hope and creative thoughts all pour into the process and we end up with a sort of thinking 'stew'. He suggests that we separate out different thinking processes by pretending to put on different coloured hats for each different process, using only one hat at a time. The colours he suggests are described below.

White hat

This is the hat that you wear if you want to assemble all the known facts and then assess them on a scale of likelihood.

You think about everything you know about a subject and then classify the information as:

always true
usually true
generally true
true more often than not
about half true
often true
sometimes true
been known to be true
never true
cannot be true.

The known facts need to be collected to make sure that nothing is overlooked before you start to think. The better the base information, the more study you make of the known facts, and the less likely you are to come to the wrong conclusion through ignorance. It is in this area that the developments in information technology are so useful. In the old days, scholars used to spend years searching libraries and reading thoroughly for the known facts before assembling these facts into a logical order. We still have to classify and judge the facts but much of the information can now be gained by operating a computer terminal.

Red hat

This hat is chosen for emotional and intuitive thinking. There is no need to justify the inclusion of intuition because we all operate within a human body which has a continual emotional tone. If you try to pretend that you 'have no emotions', it is rather like saying that you 'haven't got a temperature'. You always have a temperature whether it is high, low or normal and you always have an emotional tone whether it is excitable, gloomy or calm. The danger of not acknowledging the influence of hunches in thinking is that they will have a random and unknown effect on the final judgements. Bring this influence out into the open and then you can make sure it plays a reasonable role in reaching the final decision.

Black hat

This is the hat that is chosen for negative criticism. As soon as someone puts up a new idea we seem to be trained to whack it down again before it has even started. I agree with Edward de Bono when he says that Western society is trained to be negative in this way, to the detriment of creative thought and that this instinct often stands in the way of people working together. At school and college we seem to be encouraged to assume a right to destroy and knock down ideas but no obligation to build up new ones. 'Black hat' thinking is needed at some stages of thinking as a test to see that we are not about to carry out foolish actions. It should not be allowed at other times in case it kills off progress and originality.

Yellow hat

This hat is the opposite to the black hat. It is positive criticism and thinking with hope and optimism. An ilustration of this type of thinking might be, 'Well, I saw a good example of that working in practice'. Thinking with the yellow hat on means that we would be constructive, helpful and supportive of others if it is a group exercise and hopeful if we are on our own doing the exercise inside our heads.

Green hat

This is the colour for creativity and new ideas. I suppose that this is where plagiarism comes in. There really are very few truly original ideas. Most originality in everyday life consists of adapting a new use for an old idea; it is more innovation than being truly creative. At any rate Edward de Bono is extremely helpful in making suggestions on originality in practical thinking. He calls it 'lateral' thinking and this is usually encouraged by taking almost any step which will break set modes of thinking. We have to approach the topic from another angle to get out of a thinking rut.

Blue hat

Like the blue sky which arches over our heads, this hat is for overall thinking control. The thinking is designed to organize, control and guide all our other thinking processes, as shown in Figure 9.1.

Just as we cannot be critical unless we know something about the topic, so we cannot carry out blue hat thinking unless we have already done other types of thinking. The blue hat thinking usually finishes off the thinking process and decides what action the body or group should take. The blue hat is the managing director and the judge of the brain.

Keep this model in mind. We will use it in the next chapter which deals with problem-solving when the rolling way in which thinking and understanding link (see Figure 9.1) can be used as part of the problem-solving process.

META-COGNITIVE SKILLS

I really wish that there was a better name for this very important concept. What it means is the skill of knowing the way our own mind works. 'Self-knowledge' doesn't

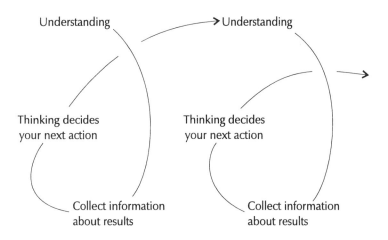

Figure 9.1 *The continuous process of learning*

137

quite hit the nail on the head, but it may help if I list the sort of things that meta-cognitive skills cover:

- how your preceptions are influenced by your own interests
- how to chunk information to gain a lot in short-term memory
- how to observe and listen
- how to store in long-term memory
- how to recall effectively
- how to study on your own
- your own set of values in your schema
- your own preferred learning style
- how to balance thinking to come to sound decisions
- how to 'day-dream' as effective forward planning
- how to think to encourage innovation and originality
- how to know your own emotions and empathize with others.

It seems that people who are in conflict with themselves have little time for other things and other people: they waste too much time on internal battles. Self-centred people appear blind to most of what is going on around them. If we can come to terms with our own strengths and weaknesses, then we have a chance of enjoying life and other people. This is why understanding our own internal mental mechanisms is such a good step in the right direction.

If you have meta-cognitive skills, then you can roll along with the certainty that you are being as effective as you are capable of being.

Notes

What is the context?
The subject of the passage was Christopher Columbus.

A picture as an advanced organizer.
The picture which acts as an advanced organizer is this:

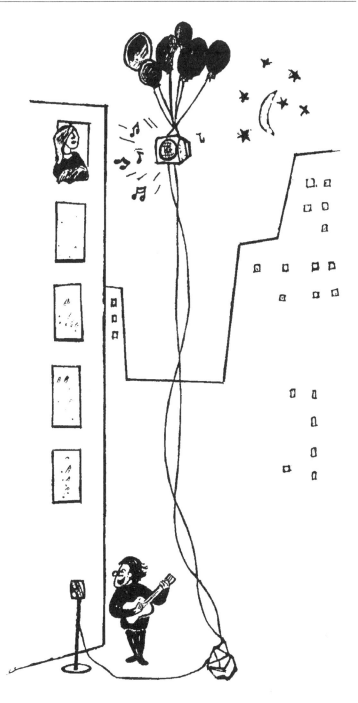

139

Chapter 10

Problem-solving

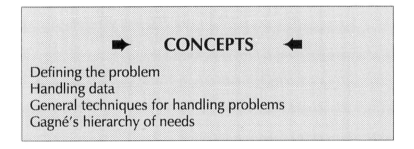

CONCEPTS

Defining the problem
Handling data
General techniques for handling problems
Gagné's hierarchy of needs

Many learning sessions end with a practical problem which the teacher sets to act as a summary of the work that has been covered and as the final check and proof that the learner has learnt. Many teachers are sad and disappointed when the learner fails to find a solution; what seemed to be clear to the teacher turns out to be muddy confusion to the student. This is a serious barrier to understanding and learning, as the whole purpose of many programmes and courses is to help learners to gain problem-solving skills in technical subjects. Let us assume that the learner has learnt all the facts and techniques required but still lacks the skills. Three things can go wrong:

- lack of skills in defining the problem clearly
- lack of technique in handling the available data
- lack of understanding the methods of problem-solving.

DEFINING THE PROBLEM

Whenever you have a goal which is blocked for any reason, such as a lack of resources or information, you have a problem. Whatever you do in order to achieve your goal is problem-solving.

The first thing to do is to clarify the problem; you need to define what you are trying to do. There are always four parts to every problem: where you begin, where you want to get to, what you can do and what you can't do. We will look at each part in the form of a question you can ask yourself and I will use management jargon for each stage because the terms are useful.

WHERE AM I NOW?

Gather together all the information you can about what is sometimes called the *initial state*. Where are you starting from? Problem-solving is rather like going on a journey and you have to define your starting point. It is no use thinking about a great solution if it turns out to be impractical because you haven't got the tools, the materials or the equipment to carry out your plans. It really isn't much of a joke when you think about what is meant by, 'Well, I wouldn't start from here'.

WHERE AM I GOING?

We have discussed goal clarity in Chapter 4. When defining a problem it is important to make sure that you know what you want to achieve and that it is what you really need. Gather together all the information about what can be called the *goal state.* Where do you want to get to? It is worth spending some thinking time on this because you do not want to waste your effort. You may work hard to solve a problem only to find yourself in the wrong place or with side effects that you did not expect.

What can I do to achieve a solution?

You must collect all the techniques, strategies and rules which can be used in the solution of a problem. These problem-solving tools are called, in management jargon, the *legal operators*: all the things you are allowed to do in the process of solving the problem.

What will prevent me from finding a solution?

The final process in defining a problem is to look at the constraints. You may not have the right tools; you may not have enough time; you may not possess the right skills. Collect all the information about the factors that govern or constrain your problem-solving tools – the legal operators. Any constraints are called the *operator restrictions*.

Here is an example to sort out the meaning of the terms. Suppose I set out to solve a crossword:

The initial state – a series of blank boxes with perhaps one or two letters in set positions.

The goal state – the whole series of letters filled in correctly.

The legal operators – words from a recognized dictionary which are the logical answers to the written clues.

The operator restrictions – existing letters, length of words, the number of spaces and so on.

═══════════ **ACTIVITY** ═══════════

Defining a problem
Think of one of your current problems. Clarify and write down the

- initial state
- goal state
- legal operators
- operator restrictions.

HANDLING DATA

The classic work of Jerome Bruner (Bruner *et al.*, 1956) gives an excellent framework for understanding the main ways in which a problem-solver can handle data. Bruner said that there were four ways of approaching problems. Each method is a useful process for problem-solving but it is the type and the amount of data to be marshalled which usually affect your choice of approach. First study each approach and then we will look at the most effective applications.

Simultaneous scanning

The problem as a whole is viewed as one single operation: all the information and known parameters are considered at one glance. This approach to handling data can only be useful if –

- the problem is very simple and there is very little information
- the problem-solver has a great deal of experience and can 'chunk'(see Chapter 2) large parts of previous experience together.

A good example of an experienced problem-solver using this technique might be a master chess player. He or she will consider the choice between two or three different approaches as a simple overall scan but each of the approaches will involve many complex linked moves on the board.

Continuous scanning

This old and trusted method of dealing with data can be summed up in the words, 'Start at the beginning and work through the material until you reach the end'. There is no doubt that you do cover all the ground by this method of data handling but it does have disadvantages.

First, the method is the slowest possible way to handle data. Second, it has no mechanism for 'highlighting' important areas and so major factors or cues may be overlooked.

Third, there is no way of looking at the problem from a different aspect and, as we shall see in the section on techniques for problem-solving, this greatly hampers originality and creativity.

I dislike lessons, lectures, speeches and instructions which are organized in this way because I feel as if I am being dragged along a remorseless, boring route. My mind wanders to lunch, fresh air or anything that will break the monotony. It is worth remembering that this type of problem-solving approach may lack motivation as well. However, this is the only way of handling data *and* making sure that nothing is overlooked.

Conservative focusing

This method is the basis of all scientific classification. When plants are being classified they are sorted into two main groups: monocotyledons and dicotyledons. The data are handled in a series of logical steps so that all known information about the plants is gradually sorted into more and more detailed categories.

Take the problem of getting from London to Paris. If you were looking at methods of travel you could put all the ways of travelling into two categories:

- in the air
- on the ground.

Then you could group all the methods of going by air into:

- by helicopter
- by aeroplane,

and further you can group by aeroplane into:

- by commercial airline
- by private flight.

In this way the data are organized into a logical classification tree and can be sifted by examining with a series of simple questions.

Focus gambling

This is the quickest method of handling data. You simply guess. If I want to go from London to Paris I will say to myself, 'What about trying the new City airport?' and then I would ring up the airport and ask about the flights. If they have good services which suit my need then the problem is solved with minimum effort. If they don't have convenient flights or they are too expensive then I will try another blind guess and I may be lucky a second time.

This method of problem-solving can be a problem in itself in the classroom. If some students come up with the right answer very quickly, it may be that they are lucky and have hit on the right answer by chance. The solution may be based on no understanding of the underlying principles at all and this causes a difficulty for the teacher.

GENERAL TECHNIQUES FOR HANDLING PROBLEMS

State space analysis

Bruner's theory of cognition classification was the basis of a popular game called 'Mastermind'. It is a small board game in which the solution can be found by building up the type of classification method described in conservative focusing.

Some problems lend themselves to this type of analysis. The correct solution can be found by constructing a logical diagram of all the possible solutions. To extend the London to Paris problem it would be possible to detail a classification system which would cover all possible parameters controlling the transport of a person from London to Paris. You would work out the framework of a classification system covering important factors like price, time, air or ground travel and then fill in examples from existing services. For example, you might search for a private flight for under £50 in the 'off-season'.

This building of a classification diagram leaves spaces which can be filled with all the possible combinations of legal operators. Some of these combinations are not feasible solutions because they fall within the operator restrictions

145

but the process of building up all the possible solutions by filling all the spaces in the structure diagram means that no solution will be left out by chance.

ACTIVITY

Using state space analysis
Take a problem and build a classification tree for all the possible solutions to the problem. You will need a large sheet of paper because these diagrams increase very rapidly as you fill in each space and the branching effect starts.

Logic diagrams

Some people are so keen on logic problems that they pass their leisure hours solving them in the same way that other people might watch television. This technique is a useful way to tackle problems when you have to organize a balance between legal operators and operator restrictions. Here is a logic problem which will show you the use of a logic diagram.

I live in Cornwall but work at the University of Greenwich. Driving alone, it is a long way to travel to work by car. My usual method of travel is from Truro railway station to Paddington and then by tube and bus, if necessary, to the university campus. I teach at two sites, Wapping in Docklands and Roehampton in South West London. It only takes 20 minutes on the tube from Paddington to the Wapping campus, but if I am heading for Roehampton, first I have to catch a tube to Putney, then travel by bus, so I cannot do the journey in less than an hour. Getting to Truro station is no problem because I can walk if no one in the family can give me a lift.

British Rail seems to set a series of hurdles when pricing its tickets. I can get an Apex fare for £39 but I can't use it before 10 o'clock and never on a Friday. I can travel on a Friday with an Advanced Super Saver which costs £45 but, like the Apex ticket, I have to book a week in advance. The normal fare is £98 but you can use both Apex and Advanced Super Savers on overnight trains provided you pay the extra £21 for a sleeper. It is very uncomfortable to sit up in the ordinary seats in the coach at the end of the sleeper train. My digs in London cost £15 a night.

Slow trains always take five hours to Paddington from Truro station but Pullman fast trains take only four hours. However, it is a long journey and I don't like to risk being late if I have to give a lecture so I always take the earlier train. I don't mind taking the risk if I am attending a meeting. Normally I have a timetable at the beginning of the semester but my head of school sometimes calls meetings at short notice and my office manager may ask me to give a lecture with little notice too.

There are four useful trains from Truro which run every day of the week. The 0555 is a Pullman and the second morning train at 0735 is a 'stopper'. The two in the evening are the 1755 which is the returning Pullman and the overnight train leaves at 2145.

This is a problem which lends itself to a logic diagram (see Figure 10.1). Here is an example of how the problem can be set out. The cheapest way to travel for any lecture or meeting at either site is broken down into train times, types of ticket, location of lecture or meeting, length of notice and day of the week. Once you know the time and the type of event you can use the logic diagram to find the lowest cost.

Analogical problem solving

In the section on insightful learning in Chapter 1 we saw that much learning is a case of recognizing something with which we are familiar. This can be summed up as, 'Hello, here comes the thing-a-me-bobs again'. Many problems are solved by taking previous experience and examples from the long-term memory store and trying to see if the new problem can be solved by using a previously-tried solution.

	LECTURE AT WAPPING	MEETING AT WAPPING	LECTURE AT ROEHAMPTON	MEETING AT ROEHAMPTON	FRIDAY	TIMETABLE	ONE WEEK	2 DAYS	APEX	A.S.A	NORMAL	SLEEPER
0555												
0735												
1755												
2145												
Apex												
A.S.A												
Normal												
Sleeper												
Friday												
Timetable												
One week												
2 days												

Figure 10.1 *A logic diagram for the travel problem*

This technique relies on finding a sound analogy. Teachers have always used this technique; indeed the technique was going strong at the time of Socrates!

STOP AND REFLECT

Do you use analogy in your teaching?
Are you sure that you don't limit your students' later study and understanding by using too rigid or too simple an analogy?
I ask this last question because it falls into the category of what I call the 'billiard ball atom'. If you teach atomic structure in terms of solid billiard balls with positive and negative charges you may get a quick early understanding of simple structure but you mess up the progression to quantum theory and quarks. There are dangers in using limited analogies in both explanations and problem-solving. However, analogies which are carefully chosen can help learning and they are widely used in problem-solving.

Synectics

This is an American term which is used for a planned system of problem-solving. There are lots of different schemes for planning group work to try to solve technical, production and organizational problems. These techniques are not well known in education but they are widely used in modern business and management.

A planned procedure for tackling a problem is laid down, rather like the procedure for brainstorming which was described earlier. The group works through each stage until an agreed solution is found. The technique can also be used by one person following the same steps. Here is a system that is designed to encourage analogous problem-solving.

There are four stages to the problem-solving process:

paradox   analogy   equivalence   unique solution.

At the paradox stage the problem is considered from the point of view of the operator restrictions. What is it about the problem which causes it to be a problem? Go right back to the beginning definition of the problem. What is blocking the achievement of your goal?

I will give you an example as we work through these stages:

> My father, who is 90, has to use a walking frame to get about. The problem is that he can't carry things about when he is using his frame. The paradox is that although he may want to fetch something or carry something around, such as his paper, while he is moving he hasn't got a hand free to carry the paper because he is using them both to hold onto the frame.

The next stage is to find an analogy. Ask yourself what this situation is like. Does this remind you of something?

> My father's situation is just like riding a bicycle. When I was young and riding my bike back from the paper shop, I couldn't hold onto a paper because I was holding on to the bicycle handles.

The next stage is to check the equivalence. Are we talking about essentially the same problem? If so, how was the problem solved in this similar situation?

> In the example the situations seem to be the same and so we can look at the solutions. These could be bicycle baskets, bags to be attached to the bicycle or a knapsack to wear on the back.

The final stage is to consider the alternative suggestions and choose the unique solution for the particular problem.

> In this example I chose the bicycle basket because a light basket for a child's bicycle was easy to fix onto the front of a walking frame.

ACTIVITY

Using a problem-solving system
This is a more effective system than you might think at first glance. Try to select a problem and work through each stage. It is better if you can work with other people but you can work through the stages on your own provided you keep to the sequence and give each stage some solid thought.

There are many different systems which have been developed for solving problems but they all have one thing in common. The system becomes more useful with practice and a group can be trained to become more skilled at finding good solutions. Some industries have management groups trained in problem-solving techniques and they benefit from the experience of working together.

One of the fastest growing research fields is cognitive psychology. Here are some recent results of work on the finding of analogies. You may find this list a useful trigger for your own problem solving by analogy.

Relation type	Definition	Analogy example
Class member	a) One term is a specific instance of a more general term	Biology:Science as opposed to Sculpture
	b) Both terms are instances of a more general class	Wolf:Dog as opposed to Tiger
Part-whole	One term is part of another	Paragraph:Sentence as opposed to Sentence alone
Order	One term follows another in time	Acorn:Oak as opposed to Bulb
Property	One term has a property or quality defined by the other	Green is used to define Emerald but not Red
Function	a) One term performs some function for or action on the other	Man:Wheat has a relationship which Knotweed does not
	b) One term performs the function defined by the other term	Ear:Hear but not Eye
Conversion	One term is made from or is the product of the other	Sail: Cloth but not Oar
Location	a) One term is located in, on or about the other often or always	Butter:Bread as opposed to Sugar

| | b) One term performs some activity in, on or about the other often or always | Train:Rail as opposed to automobile |
| Part-whole and function | One term is a part of the other and performs a specialized function | Car:Brakes as opposed to Ship |

Just as it is possible to improve thinking by practice it is possible to improve the skills of problem-solving. Here is a list of skills which improve your performance.

Associational fluency

This is the ability to make links between words and functions.

Divergent thinking

This is sometimes called lateral thinking and it is the ability to spread your thoughts about a central theme rather than follow a straight line of thoughts.

Syllogistic reasoning

This is logical reasoning from known facts and sensible premises to reach a logical conclusion which is sometimes called deductive reasoning.

Aristotle started syllogistic reasoning. There are two premises which are followed by a conclusion:

Premise one: if there is a recession the book will not sell.
Premise two: there is a recession.
Conclusion: this book will not sell.

The validity of the argument is not affected by whether the premises are true. Here is a false conclusion reached through using false premises:

Premise one: If she is a woman, then she is Aristotle.
Premise two: She is a woman.
Conclusion: She is Aristotle.

For some reason very little if any logic is taught in the English school system. We are not familiar with some classic examples of illogical thought processes. Here are some examples of where thinking can become illogical:

1. All As are Bs   – all pigs are animals
   All Cs are Bs   – all cats are animals
   Therefore all As are Cs – all pigs are cats!

2. No As are Bs   – no flowers are green
   All Cs are Bs   – all plants are green
   Therefore no As are Cs – no flowers are plants.

3. No As are Bs   – no chickens are footballers
   No Bs are Cs   – no footballers are birds
   Therefore no As are Cs – no chickens are birds.

4. No As are Bs   – no birds are mammals
   No Bs are Cs   – no mammals are reptiles
   Therefore all As are Cs – all birds are reptiles.

ACTIVITY

Testing your logic
Try out each of these logical mistakes and try to work out examples from your own subject area. Hopefully this will give you some insight into how your students can make logical errors when they are trying to solve problems.

Associative memory

Some of the earliest work on memory used to divide the process into two sections: assimilation and association. The terms are still used because they are helpful. Assimilation is the whole process of bringing in information through our senses and storing it in the procedural or functional memory. The idea of associative memory refers to the ease with which the thinker can bring similar events into use from the long-term memory. People who are skilled in this area are able to use all the previous experience of their life in solving the current problem.

Semantic flexibility

Since so much of thought is linked to language, good problem-solving skills require the ability to climb through and search amongst words easily and quickly.

Coming back to zero

One of the most difficult areas of transition between experience in the learning environment and in the real world that students have to manage is that of problem-solving. Teachers organize experience for the students so that the difficulty of the problem is graded. Easy problems are placed at the beginning of a programme, more complex problems towards the end. This makes teaching sense because you want the student to succeed and you want the student to build up to greater complexity and a greater divergence of examples. Unfortunately, life is not like that: problems come in any sequence of complexity.

The irony is that when you have tackled and coped with a series of really difficult problems you are less able to deal with something very simple. I will give you an example. Some years ago I had a big old Standard Vanguard which was overheating. Our family had very little money to spare at the time because the boys were young. I was very distressed when one garage mechanic said I needed a new engine. I couldn't afford the repair and so I took the car away and went to another garage. The second diagnosis was cylinder trouble and a third garage advised a new radiator. I was feeling quite cheerful when I took my car to a fourth garage, where the mechanic said, 'Oh yes! Splendid old cars but the water hoses are always perishing and leaking. Sorry. I will have to replace all the hoses to make sure'. He replaced the hoses and my old car ran for another 50,000 miles.

The mechanics who diagnosed more serious trouble and repairs were not bad at their jobs – they worked for good and reliable firms – but it was likely that they were stuck in the 'set' of complex problems and couldn't clear back to the 'initial state'.

This is the principal problem with problems. You must clear away any lingering thoughts about the previous problem or you will be unable to start from zero with an open mind for the next problem.

GAGNE'S HIERARCHY OF LEARNING

We have been through many parts of learning theory and have looked at a large number of theories and ideas. Like Maslow with his simple hierarchy of factors which motivate, Gagné (1956) summarized learning theories in a hierarchy too.

SIGNAL LEARNING
The establishment of a simple connection
in which a new stimulus signals
the original response

This is classical conditioning

STIMULUS-RESPONSE LEARNING
The establishment of a connection between
stimulus and response
where the new and voluntary response
satisfies some need or motive

This is operant conditioning

CHAINING
The connecting of a sequence
of two or more previously learned
motor stimulus-response connections

VERBAL ASSOCIATIONS
The learning of chains of words
which is especially important
in the learning of a language

DISCRIMINATION LEARNING
Making different responses to similar stimuli.

These are more complex thinking decisions
because of the problem of interference

CONCEPT LEARNING
Learning to make a common response
to stimuli that forms a class or category
and which may have different physical characteristics

RULE LEARNING
Putting together two or more concepts
so that a general rule or
procedural guideline can be used on different examples

PROBLEM-SOLVING
The application of old rules to
a new situation
and the process of ordered thinking
to come up with unique solutions

Figure 10.2 *Gagné's hierarchy of learning*

This is a useful summary to the introduction to learning theory. It is interesting to note that problem-solving is the most complex form of learning. You should remember this when we look at the learner in the second book in this series.

References

You will find that many of these references are quite old because this book is a summary of many theories of learning and not the latest advances in one school of psychology. If you cannot get hold of the original work you should find references to the particular theory in later publications.

Atkinson, Atkinson, Smith and Bem (1993) *Introduction to Psychology*, 11th edn, London: Harcourt Brace Jovanovich.

Atkinson, J.D. and McClelland, J.W. (1960) *Achievement Motivation*, New York: Wiley.

Bernstein, Basil (1971) *Class, Codes and Control*, London: Routledge and Kegan Paul.

Bransford, J.D. and Johnson, M.K. (1973) Considerations of some problems of comprehension. In W.G. Chase (Ed) *Visual Information Processing*, New York: Academic Press.

Bruner, J.S. *et al.* (1956) *A Study of Thinking*, New York: Wiley.

Dewey, J. (1952) *Experience and Education*, Collier Macmillan.

Claxton, Guy (1988) *Live and Learn*, Milton Keynes: Open University Press.

de Bono, E. (1970) *Lateral Thinking: A Textbook of Creativity*, London: Ward Lock.

de Bono, E. (1971) *The Mechanism of Mind*, Harmondsworth: Penguin.

de Bono, E. (1986) *Six Thinking Hats*, London: Viking.

Festinger, L. (1957) *A Theory of Cognitive Dissonance*, Stanford University Press.

Flanders, Ned (1970) *Analysing Teacher Behaviour*, London: Addison-Wesley.

Gagné, R.M. (1977) *The Conditions of Learning*, 3rd edn, Holt Rinehart and Winston.

Gardner, Howard (1985) *The Mind's New Science*, Basic Books.

Gibbs, G. (1978) *How Do I Learn?*, London: FEU.

Gibbs, G. (1988) *Learning by Doing: A Guide to Reading and Learning Methods*, London: FEU.

Hebb, D.O. (1949) *The Organization of Behaviour, a Neuro-psychological Theory*, New York: Wiley.

Honey, P. and Mumford, A. (1992) *Manual of Learning* (3rd edn), Maidenhead: P. Honey.

Keller, F.S. (1974) *The Keller Plan Handbook: Essays on a Personalized System of Instruction*, London: Benjamin.

Knowles, M. (1990) *The Adult Learner: A Neglected Species*, 4th edn, London: Kogan Page.

Kolb, D.A. (1984) *Experiential Learning – Experience as the source of Learning and Development*, NJ: Englewood Cliffs.

Maslow, A.H. (1970) *Motivation and Personality*, 2nd edn, London: Harper & Row.

Piaget, J. (1952) *The Origins of Intelligence in Children*, New York: International Universities Press.

Piaget, J. (1969) *The Psychology of the Child*, New York: Basic Books.

Rogers, C. (1951) *Client Centered Therapy*, New York: McGraw-Hill.

Rogers, C. (1970) *On Becoming a Person*, Boston, MA: Houghton Mifflin.

Stimson, N. (1991) *How to Write and Prepare Training Materials*, London: Kogan Page.

Vygotskii, L.S. (1962) *Thought and Language*, Cambridge, MA: MIT Press.

Index

active learning 110–12
arousal 96–7
attention 93–6

barriers to understanding 129–32
behaviourism 42–5
blind spot 11
Bruner, Jerome
   conservative focusing 144
   continuous scanning 143
   focus gambling 145
   simultaneous scanning 143

cognitive psychology 48–51
counselling study skills 77
cue recognition 21

de Bono's practical thinking 134–7
depth of study 69

explaining 128

Gagné's hierarchy of needs 155–6

heuristic approach 109
humanistic psychology 45–6

improving your memory 33–8
insight 22, 125

Kolb's experiential cycle 112–19

language
   as a weapon 84
   definition of 80
   Flander's interaction analysis
     87–90
   restricted 85
   specialist 82–4
   'teacher talk' 86
   understanding 81

learning opportunities 121–3
learning styles 119–20
learning to learn 68

memory
   episodic memory 30
   semantic memory 29
   short-term memory 26
   working memory 28
meta-cognitive skills 137–8
motivation
   arousal and homeostasis 63–4
   cognitive dissonance 65
   ego defence mechanism 53
   goal clarity and achievement
     64–7
   Maslow, Abraham 57–63
   reinforcement 54–6
   self-actualization 57

naive student 71
neurobiological approach 46–7

perceptual
   constancy 14
   organization 14
     continuity 16
     closure 17
     proximity 16
     similarity 15
   readiness 19
     functional fixedness 21
     knowledge and interest 19
     personality traits 19
     previous experience 19
     social and cultural interest 20
   selectivity 18
   storing perceptions 24
problem solving
   analogical 147
   associative memory 153

logic diagrams 146
state space analysis 145
synectics 149
syllogistic reasoning 152
psychoanalytic approach 41–2
promoting skill in learning and
    studying 72–7

questioning 90–91

reasoning 126–7
retrieval 31

sense organs 10
skill
    components 97–9
    demonstration 105
    job analysis 99–102
    levels of competency 107–8
    standards of work 103–5
    student practice 106

thinking 133–4

understanding 132